Ocean Glory

Ocean Glory

This is my Father's world

W. Phillip Keller

WORD BOOKS
PUBLISHER
WACO, TEXAS
A DIVISION OF
WORD, INCORPORATED

Photography by the author

Library of Congress Cataloging in Publication Data

Keller, Weldon Phillip, date
  Ocean glory.

  1. Ocean.   2.   Christian life.   I.   Title.
GC28.K44   551.4′6   79-22366
ISBN 0-8499-0459-5

To
the ocean,
with which I am deeply in love.

Contents

Acknowledgments

Thanks be given to my Father in heaven for the great joys of living by the sea . . . . for the inspiration of its glory and grandeur.

Also I am grateful for Ursula's (my wife's) enthusiasm for this book. She has shared many of my ocean days, and undertook to type the manuscript.

Bless the Lord, O my soul. O Lord my God, thou art very great; thou art clothed with honour and majesty. Who coverest thyself with light as with a garment: who stretchest out the heavens like a curtain: Who layeth the beams of his chambers in the waters: who maketh the clouds his chariot: who walketh upon the wings of the wind.

Psalms 104: 1-3

Introduction–The Pull of the Sea

All over the globe there is eternally at work the gigantic gravitational pull of sun, moon, and planets upon the oceans. It is the majestic magnetism which moves enormous, unmeasurable masses of water across the surface of the earth. With magnificent precision and uncanny predictability, titanic tides rise and fall, ebb and flow. Like the rhythmic, powerful, pulsing life of the human heart, so the oceans of the world are in constant motion within the ecosystem.

This never-resting, ever-throbbing action of the sea likewise exerts, in its turn, an incredible, undefinable pull upon human beings. It draws us with a unique attraction, which poets, philosophers, scientists, and ordinary lay people have endeavored to explain from various viewpoints. For some it is a romantic affair. For others it is purely physical and biological. And to some it is an imperative, inescapable part of life itself.

This book, in essence, is the authentic story of one man's love affair with the ocean. It has been a stirring romance, stretched out over more than half a century. During that time the sea has drawn me back again and again with an intense, irresistible magnetism. No matter where my life's work has taken me, throughout numerous countries around the world, always, ever, there has remained this strange, powerful, pulsing pull.

At least twelve full years of my life have been lived within earshot of the surf. Some of the most winsome and wonderfully rewarding times have been those when I watched the rise and fall of the tides from my front windows. Few are the hours in my career that have been more stimulating than those spent strolling, alone, along the windblown, wave-washed beaches of the world. These are precious, poignant interludes. Comingled with sun and sand and surf, with seabirds wheeling in the wind, it is there I so often know and revel in the company of my heavenly Father.

All of this may sound strange, coming from a man whose forebears were Swiss mountain people. That little landlocked country, without any coastline or open access to the sea, would scarcely seem the place from which an ocean lover would come. Even more remarkable is the fact that I was born and raised 600 miles inland from the sea. My earliest recollections of the ocean are when I first laid eyes upon the lazy lagoons and steamy mangrove mud flats near Mombasa, on Africa's east coast.

It was hardly a propitious start for what would later flower into a full-bloom love affair with oceans. The more so because of a thoroughly frightening incident that occurred the first time I stayed by the sea. I was only eight years old. My mother, modestly garbed in a huge flowing gown and great white hat, had taken a little friend and me to a small sandy cove for a swim. As boys love to do, both of us dashed bravely into the warm waters, splashing and laughing. I saw what looked like a long, slender tree limb lying in the warm waters. I grabbed at it in glee, suddenly discovering to my horror that I had a sea snake in my hand.

Even recalling it now sends shivers up and down my spine. The blood seems to drain from my brain and face, as it did in that dreadful moment of pure panic. In utter horror, white with fear, because I had grown up in a country where venomous snakes as lethal as cobras and mambas were common, I fled screaming up the beach in blind terror.

No amount of coaxing or coercion could persuade me to go near the water again during that holiday. In fact it was a distinct relief when at last we loaded our baggage on the train and headed for the hills of home.

Subsequent events were no more helpful in promoting my love for the sea. When I was ten, my parents took me with them on a trip to America. In those distant days, it required six long weeks to make the sea voyage from Mombasa to New York. I turned out to be a terrible sailor. Much of my time was spent vomiting violently over the rail or rushing below decks to the wretched washrooms that reeked of Lysol.

Repeatedly, after that, I had to traverse the oceans by ship, once, in a huge naval convoy that took ten terrible weeks to get from the Suez Canal to London. It was an appalling ordeal. We faced furious storms, especially in the Bay of Biscay, where in one severe "blow" we made only three miles of headway in a twenty-four-hour period of steaming. The North Atlantic crossing was not much better. Wild winter gales lashed and thrashed the ocean tramp on which I had booked passage. At times even her master was sure she would be sent to the bottom, when great gray seas, flecked with foam, crashed over her bow and bridge.

How we survived remains one of the many stirring sagas of the sea. When at last we limped into Boston harbor, broken and battered, I felt sure my last ties with the ocean were terminated. But the powerful, peculiar pull of the sea does not let one go that easily. You simply do not turn on your heel and walk away from the water's edge, never to return. The majesty, the might, the grandeur, and the glory of the world's oceans had begun to cast their spell upon my spirit. It was a mysterious, magnetic attraction, made up of many things.

There were the vast, open skies; the long reaches of windswept waters; the cry of the seabirds soaring in the wind; the working of the waves; the sunlight shimmering on the surface of a million moving mounds of water; the moonlight turning the ocean to beaten silver; the aroma of salt and spume and pungent ozone in the air; the roar of breakers on the beach; the heart-stopping splendor of spectacular sunrises and sunsets.

All of these and much more etched themselves indelibly upon my memory. They would draw me back to live beside the sea. Again and again and again, I would return. That is what this book is all about. It is not a technical treatise on oceanography. It is not a mariner's manual of factual information. It is a poem of praise and wonder for the ocean's glory, which I have learned to love. This is my Father's world!

Ocean Glory

He hath made the earth by his power,
he hath established the world by
his wisdom, and hath stretched
out the heavens by his discretion.
When he uttereth his voice, there is
a multitude of waters in the heavens,
and he causeth the vapours to ascend
from the ends of the earth;
he maketh lightnings with rain,
and bringeth forth the wind
out of his treasures.

Jeremiah 10:12, 13

1
Wave-Washed Strands and Windswept Sands

Encircling all of the great oceans there are a wide variety of shorelines. Their diversity and beauty make them a realm of incredible fascination. They may be gaunt gray coasts of rock and forest, where gales of sleet with storms of rain and mist shroud the coast. They may be high clay cliffs, vast grassy marshes, or mud flats grown thickly with mangroves. They may be grim, chill edges of arctic or Antarctic ice, blue and white, with towering walls from the frozen ice pack. They may be stony headlands, gravel bays, or a score of other fantastic seascapes that mark the meeting place of sea and land.

But for me, as a man, the most alluring by far are the beautiful sand beaches of the world. Not every coast has the natural topographical terrain to produce a sandy shore. But where they do occur—where waves and wind and the great ocean currents have worked for centuries on the land to fashion a strand of sand—there lies a special world between the tides.

This is *my* special domain of pure delight. Such a beach lies at the very doorstep of where I spend several months each year. My windows look out across this shining, sun-blessed strand of shifting sand. From my desk I can watch the wind working in the tough trees rooted in that sand. I can see the breezes pick up the finer particles, shifting, drifting, piling them in windrows above high tide.

It is on these sands that I listen to the surf, born in the far places of the Pacific, beat out its music on the beach. Some days it is a gentle, subdued whispering sound: merely the oscillating movement of slow swells swirling over the shore in a smooth, flowing rhythm. The foam-flecked edges of the curling swells whirl across the smoothly shining sand like graceful dancers with flowing forms.

Just last night, with the setting sun turning the sky to gold and scarlet, I stood on the shining wet sand, watching such a spectacle. The wavelets from the incoming tide would wash up smoothly, spreading themselves in hissing patterns on the flat surface. As they

17

ran in, they picked up flotsam fragments, drifting kelp strands, and bits of broken weed. These they bore gracefully in their embrace, to lay them down gently on the higher strand. There was a winsome wonderment to this working of the sea. It was a work of art. The kelp fronds lay washed and shining in exquisite patterns. They reflected the pastel shades of the setting sun upon their wave-washed fronds and stems.

This picture, and millions more like it, persisted only for a few fleeting moments. On the shore, nothing remains static. There is an eternal flux. Perpetual change transforms the pictures from hour to hour, minute to minute. The next restless, rising wave lifts, moves, alters, and refashions the scene. It reshapes the pattern, resculpts the sand. Yet equally wonderful was the realization that none of this was done in wild, discordant abandon. There was a sublime harmony and unity in every design etched upon the beach. The waves were at work in compliance with the eternal laws of the universe—moving, singing, swirling beneath the baton of a cosmic conductor.

At other times the music and movement of the surf is almost terrifying in its intensity. Under the majestic impulse of mounting winds and ocean storms, it climbs to a rising crescendo. The great walls of water boom and break on the beach in giant thunderclaps. There is the roar of tumbling water, the power of the rushing waves surging up the sand, the hissing foam, and the fury of their impact on the land.

If one goes to walk at the ocean edge when such a storm is underway, it is to walk in quiet awe and humble wonderment. It is a sobering thought to realize that some of the huge walls of water breaking on the beach were waves born several thousand miles away, across the Pacific. They are not just a phenomenon produced by a local passing storm. Some of the surf bursting on my sun-kissed beach may well have started its movement in the grim, gray storms that surge around the Aleutian Islands, off Alaska. Or, at other seasons, they may have been spawned by a tropical typhoon four thousand miles away in the South Pacific. This ocean is a mighty mass of water, within whose depths colossal currents flow, and across whose enormous breadth waves move in tre-

mendous strength.

The ocean, perhaps more than any other part of the planet, reminds us that we are an integral part of the total universe. Earth is no more a mere island of matter in space, acting independently of and detached from all other bodies, than any man or woman is an island in society. Mysterious, little-understood magnetic attractions—of the moon, the sun, the planets of the solar system, and even remote stars—exert their pull upon our seas. No, we are not alone and on our own. The rise and fall of every tide upon the beach before my door is a powerful reminder that we are all part of an enormously complex, interdependent universe.

If we are sincere in spirit, honest in heart, and open to truth, we must in intellectual integrity admit that all this remarkable interaction—of stars, sun, moon, oceans, tides, surf, sand, and man—are not mere chance. Nor is it enough to contend that, given sufficient spans of time, such intricate and mathematically precise phenomena are but the end product of pure chance. The laws of probability are prohibitively against such a supposition.

It is for this reason that when I go to walk alone upon the beach, as I do every winter day, it is with a genuine sense of sublime awe upon my spirit. There steals over me again and again the acute, intense, undeniable awareness: "Oh, God, my Father, You are here! This is but a fragment of Your exquisite artistry, Your magnificent mind; expressed to me in terms I can understand!"

My finite comprehension of the enormous expanses of outer space and of the interstellar systems may be strained and straightened beyond my ability to understand. But when the gravitational pull of the moon lifts 10 billion tons of water 10 feet on a rising tide and sends it bursting across my beach, I can grasp a little of the greatness of God. I may not be able to fully fathom what it means when astronomers tell me the light from some distant star, traveling at one-hundred-eighty-six-thousand miles a second, has taken four thousand years to reach my eye. But I can lay hold of the loveliness of our Lord when I see that same clear, silver starlight shining on the edge of the surf that breaks endlessly before my door. No human hands have moved those waters; no human ingenuity has arranged this glory. It is from God, my Father.

Between a stretch of sand and a man there gently develops a beautiful intimacy which only those who have lived on a beach can understand. It is something more than the mere interaction and response to physical elements of sea, sky, sun, wind, and water. It is more than the delicious sensation of feeling soft, warm, resilient sand trickle between the toes. It is more than the salty tang of seawater tingling on the skin after a swim. It is more than the warm caress of sunshine on the cheeks. It is beyond the stimulating sense of well-being that sweeps across human senses in contact with the ocean.

It is best defined as a spiritual response to something very much greater than ourselves: an awareness that here man is in intimate contact with an earth system which he cannot tame or control. He is in touch with tremendous forces and elemental energy, over which he has no dominion. The vast sweep of the ocean, its restless currents, its eternal movement, its never-ceasing action, apart from and independent of man, humble his spirit.

This element of comingled love and respect for the sea is ever apparent, even in the hardiest of seafaring people. Though the ocean draws them to its heaving bosom with magical mysticism, they always respond to its overtures with a solemn sense of quiet, inner reverence.

It matters not whether it be the tough, rugged West Coast fishermen of Oregon, Washington, and British Columbia setting out to sea for the silver hordes of Pacific salmon, or a Samoan gliding softly across a coral lagoon in the mellow moonlight. Because their lives are bound up intimately with the sea and their homes are perched upon its windswept strand, they regard it with comingled awe and affection. They learn to read its writing on the sand. They can catch the messages it bears from the dark and distant reaches of the outer ocean. They can sense its changing moods and mighty movements.

This art and skill of understanding the sea does not come in one day, one week, or one year. It takes a whole lifetime of learning. It calls for humility of heart, openness of spirit,

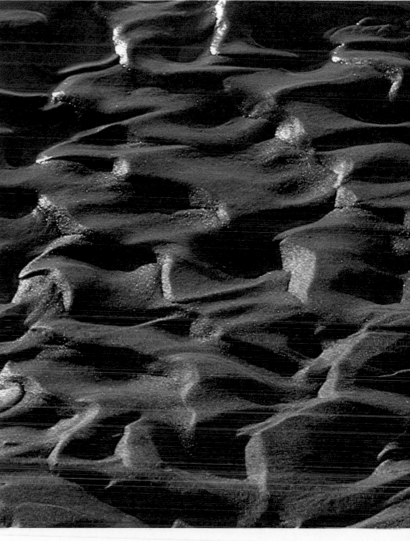

and a gracious willingness to receive what the ocean can teach us earth children.

I would like to share with the reader some of the simple yet profoundly eternal principles the sea has shared with me. For I come to walk upon its shore open to its eternal wisdom, eager to discover some new and inspiring insight into life.

Each fresh dawn, as I set out to hike along the beach, I am astonished at its newness. It is the same strand I tramped along yesterday—superficially. There is still the great arching bay that runs from the broken headlands of rock in the west to the gorgeous high cliffs of orange clay on the east. There are still the same tranquil Channel Islands rising out of the Pacific to the south, like giant whales baring their backs to the sun. There are still the tall, graceful, fan palms blowing in the wind and the gorgeous Monterey pines silhouetted starkly against the red and rising sun. There is still the sturdy ice plant blanketing the sand just above high tide. There are still the alluring cries of the cormorants, pelicans, gulls, and curlews that wheel and call in the wind above the waves.

But in the face of all this apparent sameness, the ocean verge is never ever the same two mornings in succession. As I step upon its sand, the incredible sensation of being the first man to ever set the sole of his foot upon this particular strand overwhelms me. Never before have the uncountable millions of minute grains of sand been arranged in exactly this order. The sand lies clean—swept, polished, immaculate. Every trace of every track and footprint and mark made yesterday has been erased by the night tide. What my gaze falls upon in the early hours of the dawn is a new sheet of shifting parchment, upon which will be inscribed the passing events of a new chapter in a new day.

This comes home to my heart with enormous impact. Each dawn of each day is a new beginning in life. A fresh page has been turned and is waiting to have written upon it the passing story of my days. What imprint will be left upon this brief chapter of my all-too-short life? What impress for good and for God will be left upon the shifting sand of my brief life span? Each new day brings a wave-washed sheet of time, upon which something of eternal worth may or may not be etched. What am I doing with it?

Even though yesterday may have been less than truly beautiful; even though yesterday the flotsam and jetsam of my fevered day may have been flung upon the shore of my experience; even though yesterday the tracks and footprints left upon the sand of my passing hours may have been tangled, twisted, and even unsure; even in spite of all their confusion, today can be different. Today I can start again. Today, in company with my Lord, I can write a fresh chapter.

That is the graciousness of my God. It is the generosity of my heavenly Father. He who forms and fashions the sea also forms and fashions the shape of my days. He gives me new opportunity, every morning, to inscribe better today than I did either yesterday or ten thousand other yesterdays before that.

Life need not be seen as a sad story of ongoing failure or despair. It can be the stimulating saga of endless new beginnings with my God. This is part of its grandeur, a part of its glory.

Another remarkable principle that the ocean beach has impressed upon my spirit is one shaped by the action of the waves upon sand. I see it repeated a hundred thousand times, when I walk softly between the tides. It is there for any passerby to see. Yet most of us have never been open or receptive to it.

Every wave or wavelet that surges across the sand seems to run up the beach in threatening fashion. The water foams and froths ominously. It comes swishing up the

sand, hissing menacingly. It seems intent on shifting and sweeping everything before it. No matter how or where I walk, the ocean waves are always at work, spreading themselves in a widening wash of foam and bubbles that break about me.

Yet, mysteriously, wondrously, incredibly, I have seen those same threatening waves come to a quiet end. Their energy spent, they simply sink into the sand. The water not soaked up recedes gently, to be reclaimed by the next incoming wave. The threatening presence is lost and dissipated in the matrix of the great white beach. Only tiny bursting rainbow bubbles and a vanishing fleck of foam remain to remind one of the menace.

It seemed so real, so overwhelming, so all-engulfing. Yet it came to nothing.

Life, too, is like that. So many of the events or things we fear often come to nothing. Initially they may appear, like a rising wave on the sea, intent on sweeping right over us. We are sure they will engulf us in calamity and chaos. We are terrified at times that they will fling us off our feet, to toss us up, crumpled and broken, on the beach of life.

Yet again and again, like waves that run out of energy, to spend themselves softly on the sand, the threats of our days fade away. They look so menacing, they appear so formidable; we want to turn and run from them. Yet time tames most of them. They dissolve into nothing.

Those of us who go to ramble often on the sand quickly learn the lesson of walking among the waves. I love this aspect of my hours beside the sea. There is a joy, a gaiety, a strange sense of challenge and adventure to making one's way along the surf's edge. It is a fine line one treads between the waves, ever expecting to be engulfed, yet finding safe footing on the seabed.

The older I become, the more apparent this principle is in life. We look back across the long years and see where a thousand waves of despair and discouragement threatened to engulf us in their overwhelming ferocity. At times, as events or circumstances came rushing in upon us, we were sure we would be caught up and crushed in their terrifying vortex. But again and again our worst fears were unfounded. The threatening menace spent itself upon the sand of time, and we were left untouched, unharmed.

This, too, is part of the gracious goodness of our Lord. Often, as I stroll on the sands between the breakers, I am reminded of those gracious words Christ shared with His disciples: ". . . In the world ye shall have tribulation: but be of good cheer; I have overcome the world" (John 16:33).

Not that the great breaking waves of life are counteracted in some cataclysmic crises. No, rather that in and by His own quiet arrangement of our affairs, the rushing waters simply subside into the sands of time around us, leaving us untouched and unscathed.

With refreshing joy and wonder, the words of the Lord to His ancient people come sweeping into my soul with great reassurance:

> . . . Fear not, for I have redeemed thee—I have called thee by thy name, thou art mine. When thou passest through the waters, I will be with thee; and through the rivers, they shall not overflow thee . . . .
>
> Isaiah 43:1, 2 ASV

The great beaches of the world are often of striking and diverse colors. It is the basic material from which they have been formed that determines their texture and color. I have walked for hundreds and hundreds of miles on golden sands all around the globe. The interminable surge of the seas and wash of the waves has reduced the rock along the coast to giant strands of gorgeous ocean sand. Many of the beaches are gold; others are white, pink, black, or green.

Yet these great sweeping stretches of pulverized stone, coral or lava are never static. They are being shifted and shaped inexorably by the gigantic pressures of their ocean world. In a single raging storm, a fierce blow can rage and ravage the sand, moving millions of tons from one part of the beach to another. Again and again, I have been astonished to find miles of beach literally cut away to a depth of two or three feet in a single night.

The combined forces of high tide and powerful onshore currents, with their thundering breakers, will pick up and transport ten thousand tons of sand a mile or more in a single change of tide. This stripping of the shore to rebuild it elsewhere goes on relentlessly.

Where I often walk, it is not uncommon to come out in the morning to find the ocean edge nothing but a boulder-strewn beach. It is a bare-boned rock bed, where a man can progress only with great difficulty by leaping from stone to stone, each stone glazed with lowly marine growth, shining wet, lying green or gray in the sun.

A week later the same beach will be covered in golden sand, deposited there to a depth of several feet. Borne and carried on the capricious ocean currents, it is spread smooth and shining, as if laid down by a master landscape artist.

It is in this constant movement of the sea and shore that the wind, too, is at work.

Depending upon the titanic ocean storms and planetary weather systems that encircle the globe, the winds off the sea erode and sculpt the shore with enormous energy.

Not only do the winds shift and move mountains of water in wave action, but also they actually pick up sand and grit that is then borne landward. So fierce and ferocious and continuous is the wind on some beaches that it piles up dunes of sea sand miles inland. The blowing particles of weathered rock and stone act as a rough, air-blasted abrasive that strips off the soil, tears away trees, shreds vegetation and buries one succeeding shoreline beneath another.

I vividly remember camping on a remote and lonely beach in Mexico when a severe sandstorm developed on the shore. So fierce and violent were the wind gusts that only by moving my vehicle down into the lee of a deep draw and turning its tail to the wind did it manage to survive the storm. Even then, the velocity of the wind-driven sand was sufficient to strip all the paint from any exposed metal. Every corner and crack of the vehicle was packed solid with flour-fine grit. And it took an entire day of hard, tedious labor to remove the sand from the engine, where it had been blown in and deposited in solid masses by the blinding storm.

Tempestuous winds of this wild nature will steadily build dune upon dune. There are strips of shoreline on the Oregon coast where entire successions of forest have been buried, one beneath the other. Lowly, tough, hardy beach grasses may briefly bind the shifting sand until a few stunted, misshapen trees strike root. For a short spell the vegetation may hold the beach against the onslaught of the wind, but eventually the moving sand will again engulf the struggling trees. Remorselessly, it will begin to bury them beneath its burden of sand and silt. Finally they are entombed, swept over, haunted by the howling gales and whining winds that seldom relent. In all of this there lies a somber, startling lesson. It makes me pause and marvel.

Along the beach I see and sense a dynamic microcosm of all of life. From the dawn of time—geologic time, when the first gigantic tides of earth swept inland on raging floods that covered thousands of miles of coastal plains—the biota has ever been in flux. Here I discern and discover that nothing remains the same. There is everywhere about me change, cataclysmic change. The shifting sands, the drifting dunes, the sea-rasped rocks, the chiseled coastline, the wind-wracked trees all declare eloquently that here the only constant is *change*.

We speak glibly and rather facetiously of the eternal seas, but they are in truth not eternal nor enduring. Like the great mountain ranges of the world, so the oceans overwhelm man with their might and mass. But they are not enduring. They are inexorably subject to change and movement and motion.

This truth comes home gently but surely to those of us who love the sea, who respond to its winsome call, who have fallen under its unique fascination. We sense that, at best, we are but pilgrims, passersby, wanderers who come briefly for the short span of our few years to live at the ocean edge.

All of us are transients. The tides, the waves, the wayward winds, the passing storms, the wheeling seabirds, the shifting restless sands, the schools of fish, the short-lived grasses and trees of marsh and dune are here but briefly. Is there no eternal meaning or

message here for our questing spirits? Are we all but bare fragments of material, moved and shifted only in response to the physical, chemical, and biological forces around us? Is there no sense, meaning, or purpose for my short sojourn upon this planet that is hurtling through space? Are my years and thoughts and impressions to be carried away like bits of flotsam on the tides of time? Is there no direction to the deep and profound stirring of my spirit as I stroll by the sea?

Yes, there is. Deep does call to deep. There sweeps over my soul again and again the phrase "Oh, be still, quiet, alone, silent and *know* that I am God."

All about me there may be the ebb and flow, the rise and fall of changing seasons, changing scenes, a changing world. "But You, oh, my Father, remain ever the same. You, oh, Lord, are from everlasting to everlasting."

The ancient psalmist put this wondrous assurance into the following lines:

> O Lord, how manifold are thy works! in wisdom hast thou made them all: the earth is full of thy riches. So is this great and wide sea, wherein are things creeping innumerable, both small and great beasts.
>
> Psalms 104:24, 25

> The glory of the Lord shall endure for ever: the Lord shall rejoice in his works.
>
> Psalms 104:31

As the tides change, as the winds veer from point to point on the compass, as the sand creeps across the coast, as the clouds cross the sky, there comes again and again this vibrant, joyous assurance to the spirit of God's child: "Oh, Father, You are here! You are eternal! You are sure and steadfast! Against this glorious, scintillating backdrop of sea and sky and shore, *You* stand strong and steadfast. In *You* my confidence is calm and sure. In *You* my heart glows bright with hope. *You* are forever and forever!"

It has been my great privilege and long-remembered joy to spend unforgettable interludes along some of the ocean's finest beaches. The snow-white sands of the Indian Ocean on Africa's eastern seaboard, from the Cape of Good Hope to Cape Guardafui in Somalia, have cast their spell upon me. Arab traders for uncounted centuries pushed their *dhows* on these shining shores when they went inland, searching for black slaves and white ivory. I have hiked for miles along the great, open, surf-pounded beaches of Australia and New Zealand. Here the southern oceans, in their gigantic sweep around the land masses, have fashioned miles and miles of windswept sands. In places of the remote outreaches, a man's footprint may not be seen from one month to another.

In blazing, brilliant contrast, the beautiful beaches of southern California, Florida, the East Coast of the United States, the Mediterranean, and the ocean islands are sometimes alive and swarming with thousands upon thousands of human visitors. Those who come by the millions to such strands are generally in search of sunshine, open vistas, and the exhilaration of ocean air. The warm weather, the blue waters, the golden sunlight, the soporific influence of wind and waves work wonders in the well-being of those who come on holiday.

But over and beyond all of this, there remains an aspect of the wave-washed strands that has moved me beyond words. It is the dimension of dynamic, ever-changing beauty, so fragile, in the details of the sand itself. It is a part of the windswept shores which cannot be seen from a distance or understood, in a remote or detached manner, from afar.

This is the intricate beauty and special splendor that wind and water work in sculpting sand. Here are three elemental materials, all in motion, each acting upon the other. Wind

is moving air. Waves are moving water. Sand is moving land. As they each come under the impulse of one another, we discover patterns and designs of exquisite charm inscribed on the shore.

One of my favorite times to take a tramp along the tide line is at the ebb. If the sea is down and the waves are receding in gentle, graceful arcs, there is left behind a fretwork of fantastic patterns. These designs in the sand equal anything ever etched on the finest British bone china by a master craftsman.

If the light is low in the sky, these delicate drawings in the sand stand out in bold relief. Many of them are chiseled in the surface sand by rivulets of receding water that drain across the beach. Very often their form is like that of a winter forest standing in stark ranks, stripped of leaves, with bare branches and bulky butts. The patterns are perfectly proportioned. They are not some distorted or contorted convolutions that call for a bizarre imagination to detect their design. They are exquisite, natural sand pictures.

The surprising thing to me is the brevity of their beauty. Some are drawn and die within a few short seconds. The next wave washing up the strand will erase them in a moment. Such artistry, such intricacy, such elegance—repeated ten thousand times ten thousand times—unseen and unobserved by any human visitor! These designs are like the rose that blooms and wastes its beauty on the desert air. We might well ask ourselves why so much artistry passes unnoticed upon the planet.

It is not the sand alone that responds this way to the moving water. In the foam and froth left behind every passing wave and wavelet, there are gorgeous, glowing types of embroidery that garnish the beach. One has to be very alert and intent to see these short-lived patterns. They, too, have only the briefest duration before their bubbles burst, to disappear into nothingness.

Millions upon millions of times, in any single day, the sea will cast this delicate lacework of rainbow bubbles across the sand. Only the sharp-eyed seabirds feeding in the shallows—the sandpipers, curlews, sanderlings, whimbrels, and willet—are in intimate contact with the frothy foam that is swirling elegantly about their feet. Like a divine dance of supernatural design, they move back and forth across the stage of wave-washed sand, in flowing motions of sublime rhythm and harmony.

Then there is the graceful movement of sand particles under the gentle pressure of the wind. They form shifting, drifting designs of graceful shape behind and around every stone, rock, shell, stalk of grass, or bit of flotsam flung on the beach. None of this is accidental or erratic. Grain upon grain grows steadily into sea sketches that are shaped eternally by the interaction of a planet spinning in space, by the majestic pull of the moon and the impulse of stars that are millions of miles away.

None of this is purely chance. None of this is merely blind coincidence. Each is an exquisite, intimate reminder that I live and move and have my being in a gorgeous environment ordered by a loving, caring, gracious Father. This is His world. He designed it. He set it in motion. He sustains it.

As I stroll softly on the ocean strand, my spirit is still serene in His close company. I am awed by the beauty about me. It is His deliberate design.

Where were you when I laid
the foundations of the earth?
Tell me, if you know so much.
Do you know how its dimensions were
determined, and who did the surveying?
What supports its foundations,
and who laid its cornerstone,
as the morning stars sang together
and all the angels shouted for you?
Who decreed the boundaries of the seas
when they gushed from the depths?
Who clothed them with clouds
and thick darkness,
and barred them by limiting
their shores, and said,
"Thus far and no farther
shall you come, and here shall
your proud waves stop!"?

Job 38:4–11 lb

2

Sea Cliffs and Rocky Coasts

Most of my ocean-edge days have been spent on rugged shorelines, where gaunt sea cliffs, gravel bays, rocky headlands, and grim gray stone comprised the coast. These shores do not have the open sweep of wide, windswept space that is generally associated with wave-washed strands of sun-kissed sands. But they do have a bold, wave-battered, ocean-beaten beauty that attracts our attention by their grim, wild glory.

These rock-ribbed ocean coastlines are often stern, sometimes very forbidding. In many places the native forest and vegetation grow in dense thickets down to the very edge of high tide. A comingled mass of trees, shrubs, and salt-tolerant plants form an almost-solid stand of well-nigh impenetrable growth clinging to the rain-soaked land.

In many of these coastal regions, there is a steady succession of storms that come roaring and raging in off the sea. They sweep inland rank on rank, bearing heavy squalls of rain, banks of fog, clouds of mist, and a never-ending dampness that saturates the shore. Some of these coastlines are deeply indented with deep fjords, forbidding headlands, wave-lashed rocks that jut from the sea floor like rotten old dragons' teeth, which gnash and froth with sea foam.

Some of these shores are stark and striking. Here the tides crash and thunder on the rocks, as though caught up in deadly combat with the land. It is as if the seas are determined to destroy the land against which they hurl themselves in gray and green ranks of fury. Wave upon wave mounts an attack, to go rushing against the rock, which trembles and sometimes shatters under the powerful impact of the ocean's might.

I have stood on the rocky headlands only a few yards behind my home at Silver Spray Ranch, watching winter storms that simply swept one's breath away. So fierce was the force of the wind, so monstrous the might of the great gray seas, that a man could not speak for sheer awe and wonder.

/37

Some of those giant waves had been generated in the farthest regions of the dark, chill, gray North Pacific. Without islands or land masses to obstruct their movement, they swept across three thousand miles of open ocean, to crash and vent their vehemence on this verge of coastline. As I stood on the wet headlands, where rain and spray and flecks of wind-blown foam flushed back into the sea, the bedrock would shudder, trembling beneath my feet with the immense impact of the sea.

In giant storms, the pressure of an ocean beating on solid stone can mount to more than 60,000 pounds to the square foot. That is the awesome equivalent of well over 30 tons of impact to one square foot of rock surface. Unless the rock is part and parcel of the very foundation formations, it cannot long endure such battering and abuse. Some portion of it will break loose, to be flung against the shore and serve as a giant battering ram that is caught up in the waves, to grind and rumble against other boulders in the surf.

This explains in part why some of the most-elaborate seawalls, ocean harbors, and coastal installations simply do not survive great storms. There have been instances where blocks of cement, concrete, and reinforcing steel weighing more than a thousand tons have been torn loose, broken up, and shattered by relentless ocean storms.

The less obvious reason is, of course, the simple physical fact that in deep water any submerged object becomes increasingly bouyant, to the extent of the weight of the water it displaces. A giant boulder on the seabed, or a huge block of concrete below high water, is not nearly as heavy or immovable as we might imagine. The hydraulic action of the mighty inrushing waters that thunder and roar over the rocks lifts, shifts, and splits stone, concrete, and steel with impunity and disdain.

Again and again I have stood silently in awe beside a battered, broken seawall or shattered harbor wall. The immense power that pulverized the best of man's endeavors likewise pulverizes my human pride. The skill, science, and engineering expertise that were combined to try and tame the sea came to naught. Only a twisted, torn reminder of man's insignificance remains.

At such moments, there steals softly over my spirit those solemn strains from the Psalms:

> O Lord our Lord . . . When I consider thy heavens, the work of thy fingers, the moon
> and the stars, which thou hast ordained; What is man, that thou art mindful of him? and
> the son of man, that thou visitest him?
>
> Psalms 8:1, 3, 4

This same sensation has always engulfed me whenever it has been my special pleasure to tramp a winding trail along the top of some towering sea cliffs. Such cliffs occur all over the world. Some of them have been made famous in poetry and prose. Others have found their way into folklore, songs, and the ballads of their countrymen.

Perhaps the most famous of this twentieth century was the deeply moving lyric, "There'll be bluebirds over the white cliffs of Dover." The song spoke to the deepest sentiments in the spirits of millions of people locked in the blackness and darkness of World War II. It gave cheer and spoke comfort to men in combat, who hoped and prayed and waited patiently for the return of peace. It expressed the deep desire for the days when the sun would shine again, the seas of strife would be smooth and safe once more, and the bluebirds of happiness could again fly freely over the war-ravaged coasts of the earth.

The giant sea cliffs of the ocean's edge are places of enormous interest and beauty. There is a comingled aura of grandeur and intimacy about them. In some places they are powerfully impressive. Their towering ramparts, standing tall and stark above the sea, give the impression of a formidable fortress under siege from the thundering battering rams of ocean breakers beating against their bases.

It is to such places that I have come again and again for refreshment of mind, inspiration of spirit, and rejuvenation of body. One incident especially stands out clearly in my memory, etched there by the excruciating events of the time.

I had been sent on an extended writing and photographic assignment that took me to some twenty-nine countries around the globe. It had been an exhausting ordeal. Arranging transportation from place to place; living among all sorts of strange people; sleeping in nearly a hundred different hostelries; eating foreign foods and sometimes drinking from unsanitary sources; trying to communicate in strange, unknown languages; transacting my travel arrangements in unfamiliar currencies, had all combined to bring me to the very verge of a total collapse. It was precisely at this point that my itinerary called for a brief halt in Tangiers, Morocco.

Fortunately for me, the family with whom I found lodging sensed immediately my utter exhaustion and need of rest. They lived near the sea, facing the wild Atlantic. In love, compassion, and deep understanding, for three days in a row, the lady of the house packed me a picnic lunch of crisp French bread, fresh cheese, and a bottle of homemade orange juice. With this in hand, camera over my shoulder, and binoculars in pocket, she sent me off to the sea cliffs.

It saved my sanity.

It restored my sense of repose and balance.

It refreshed my body in a remarkable manner.

I would leave the little house on the hill and wind my way through the colorful streets, with their Spanish villas. Along the way local Moroccans, with their little donkeys, would be threading the dusty trails with sacks of grain, loads of firewood, and bundles of fruit or vegetables destined for local markets.

Some of their little paths wound happily along the edge of the high cliffs above the Atlantic. There I would sit quietly in the tall grass, letting the sea wind off the Atlantic run its fingers through my hair. I would relish the pungent, powerful ozone in the air, inhaling deeply of its delicious fragrance. I could taste the salt of the sea spray that burst up from the dark black rocks below me. Its tang was strong upon my tongue and lips. As I lay stretched out in the warm Moroccan sun, I felt the caress of the sea air upon my cheeks and chest.

As I looked out across the never-ending gray green expanse of the heaving Atlantic, my soul was uplifted in hope. Those giant seas stretched three thousand miles around the planet, to touch the far coasts of my own distant homeland. It was a bond between us, and in that bond I found a quiet reassurance.

Gently, quietly, surely, sun and sea and wind off the water did their gracious work in calming my strained and weary person. The ocean realm has this peculiar power to put us right again. It has the remarkable capacity to breathe new hope and life and inspiration into our struggling spirits. It has the potency to revitalize our vision and restore our view of life.

As day followed day, I found fresh courage and vigor to climb up and down the precarious, twisting trails that wound across the cliffs. It was some of the most-picturesque scenery imaginable. The red and brown rocks; the dark green trees clinging to the cliff face; the blue, blue desert skies; the white lacework of ocean waves; the great green waters of the Atlantic; all combined to compose seascapes of breathtaking beauty.

Here I would wander by the hour, lost in total joy and wonderment. Overhead, seabirds wheeled in the updrafts of air rising against the cliff faces. Their flight was sure and swift and smooth. Along the beaches, young stalwart Moroccans, stripped to the waist, their strongly muscled torsos glistening in the sun like sculptured Greek gods, were fishing from the rocks. There was no way we could communicate, except by friendly smiles, sign language, and the comingling of our carefree spirits.

This was their world, their home, their shoreline by the sea; yet they were happy and generous enough to share it with a total stranger—a stranger who had come to their sea cliffs weary and worn and wasted, but who soon would leave light in heart, remade in mind and body.

I learned to love that ocean edge with a surprising intensity. I would linger there as long as there was light enough from the setting sun to show me the trail up the cliffs. And at close of day, as the westerly sea turned red, there leaped fresh hope within my heart that in a few more weeks I, too, would be across that great ocean and home again. The traveling would be over. The strain of strange places and strange faces would be behind me. The stress of meeting deadlines and finding transportation would be gone, and once more I could walk gently along the cliffs of home. For, in truth, what I had found in this faraway place was a home away from home.

There is in the ocean a remarkable bond that encircles all the globe. Its waters, though arbitrarily divided by man into separate seas, are really one. This flowing water, which is ever in flux, covers roughly three-quarters of the planet. It is in no sense static or stagnant. It is eternally active, ever in motion, relentlessly flowing with formidable force in great ocean currents. Yet it binds and unites all of the earth in a single unit.

The oceans encircle, touch, and caress every continent, every land mass, every island, every rock that protrudes from the sea floor. The ocean has this great glory of unifying the globe, shaping its coasts, tempering its climate, and in general contributing to the total environment in which life survives and thrives.

I can never stand alone high on a sea cliff, with the ocean roaring on the rocks below me, and not sense an overwhelming wave of genuine gratitude sweep through my spirit. There engulfs me the simultaneous sensations of my own insignificance and the glorious grandeur of the entire globe of which I am a minute part. There is imparted to me during these quiet interludes the indelible, irrefutable impression that "This is my Father's world."

Not only is there in it the moving, stirring, sublime majesty of mighty seas, but also the minute, heartwarming details of the exquisite artistry and care that have been bestowed on all living creatures who reside here.

Just last evening I went to walk at the foot of the orange brown sea cliffs beside my home. The late sun was slanting in golden shafts from beneath the clouds. It had been a misty, foggy, damp day, even for the curlews, pelicans, and cormorants. The latter had been diving for fish in the breakers most of the day.

Suddenly I watched one, then another, then another of the sleek, slender-necked birds rise from the water and soar up to the sun-warmed cliffs. With surprising precision, they alighted on the vertical face of the bluff, perching precariously on tiny toeholds in the dark brown clay. There they preened their sea-sodden plumage, stretching their wings full spread to catch the last warmth of the setting sun. It was all they needed to fit them for their night fishing. Ocean cliffs could contribute as much well-being to weary cormorants as to a weary man. And all of us rejoiced together.

It is along the great ocean cliffs that the inexorable and relentless power of the sea can best be measured by man. The collapse of the undermined land sends millions of tons of soil, rock, and debris tumbling down to the toe of the bluffs. It is quickly caught up in the wash of the waves. There the finer silt and less-stable soil is immediately carried away in the ocean currents, to be deposited as marine silt on the seabed. Some offshore continental shelves lie deep beneath a layer of mud and muck that has been extracted by erosion from the ocean edge.

So remorseless are the ravages of the sea along some exposed coasts that, in a single season of storms and high tides, fourteen or fifteen feet of coastline will be cut away. Testimony to this never-ending loss of land to the sea can be found in historical records showing that entire coastal villages and communities have been gradually washed away and lost to the ocean tides.

I have tramped for miles along the beautiful beaches that are surmounted by gorgeous sun-kissed cliffs on the southern coast of California. Here and there in my rambles I find somber reminders that this great Pacific Ocean really is not always that *pacific.* Collapsed seawalls, broken stairways of concrete, twisted wreckage of rusting metal pipes or steel girders, torn-up trees, uprooted rails, shattered buildings—all bear mute witness to the restless work of the sea.

The rising and falling tides, the eternal impact of water on stone, the gnawing and grinding of boulders against basement formations, the rasping erosion of sand- and rock-laden waves chisel away at the cliffs night and day. Slowly, slowly, but ever so surely, they are undercut. Then in some fierce blow, with rain beating against the sodden banks, the whole structure will start to shift. The end is a thundering, slithering mass of material that slips into the sea.

One spot, where I especially love to stroll, this attrition of the sea on land lies ever before me in stark reality. Imbedded in the sand are huge slabs of concrete walls, built to protect the cliffs. They lie twisted, broken, wave-worn, lodged at crazy angles to the surf. Here, too, there are once-proud gravestones, slabs of chiseled marble, and broken Grecian columns that once were the pride of their owners. Now they lie buried in shifting sand, garlanded with seaweed, and grown over with barnacles.

All of this reminds me again and again that there is nothing permanent upon the planet. All is change. On every hand there is constant movement and refashioning. Yet, strange to say—as with mountains, so with ocean bluffs—I have found here moments of great repose and enormous uplift of spirit.

There is something very comforting, very reassuring for us human beings in the company of cliffs. For one thing, they have the capacity to close out all the clamor and cacophony of our contemporary world. A man or a woman who seeks solitude, who longs for a spot in which to think "long thoughts," who seeks temporary relief from the relentless tension of our times can find it in the company of the sea cliffs.

Again and again it has impressed me deeply how these are the spots where one sees young people, often alone, occasionally in company with another, lost in reflection and quiet repose. If one walks along the foot of the bold bluffs, all other sounds but those of the sea are shut out effectively. There remains only the surge of the surf, the wild cries of the seabirds, the whispering of the wind. These are all music—soothing music, soporific music—that stills our souls and calms our spirits.

Across the long years of my own life, certain ocean bluffs and special sea cliffs have become among the most-precious spots on earth. Again and again I have come there, seeking healing for my body, seeking wholeness for my emotions and mind, seeking inspiration and enthusiasm for my spirit. In all honesty and sincerity, I can say without equivocation that the ocean has never disappointed me. A great part of her grandeur and her glory lies in this unique and remarkable capacity to restore wholeness to our lives.

/47

I have certain little coves, quiet sandy stretches—sun-blessed, sun-kissed fragments of storm-beaten beach, tucked away at the toe of great cliffs—where I often go to find peace and rest and refreshment. Never have I been refused that which I sought from the sea. Many of my books and some of my best writing has been achieved under her gentle, gracious spell.

I recall vividly those desperate, dark, sad days when my life partner, my beloved and beautiful first wife, lay dying beneath the dreadful ravages of cancer. There was nothing more that medicine, science, or the physician's skills could do to support her. She would request, in her extreme weakness, that I take her down by the sea.

Bundling her up in blankets, I would settle her against some ocean-borne log, where she was partially protected from the wind. Sitting there side by side, hand in hand, we would spend a quiet hour or two, letting the sea breezes caress her sallow cheeks, letting the ocean sounds soothe her spirit, listening to the call of the quail from the broom bushes on the bluffs behind us, watching the immaculate white-and-gray gulls wheel against the blue sky.

Those were precious moments for two people face-to-face with death on the doorstep of their lives. They were intimate interludes, among the last we would share before she was called away to that farther shore, where there would be no more pain or tears or parting. In those gentle times by the sea beneath fair winds, our Father used the ocean's glory to soothe our wounded, weary spirits.

After she was gone, I would return often to those same spots, to sit quietly and reflect upon the gracious goodness of my God. In humble gratitude, my heart has been uplifted there, for in the eternal ebb and flow of the tides, I am reminded again of the eternal

faithfulness of my heavenly Father. His forthright, unequivocal commitment to me, as His child, ever is: "Lo, I am with you always!"—whether here or on that fair strand of life beyond this scene.

He has made good on His promises to me, for across the succeeding years, He has brought into my life a second lovely lady. She, too, is drawn to the sea and loves it. She, too, finds joy and inspiration and tranquility along its sun-blessed beaches. Just yesterday, Valentine's Day, she lay stretched out beside me on the golden sands, adorned in her beautiful snow-white bikini. The gentle glow of her suntanned cheeks, the warm, happy sparkle of her soft brown eyes, the lithe gracefulness of her lovely form, the gentle smile on her face—all bespoke a woman at peace with her world and in love with her man. And both of us knew we were fortunate beyond measure. Our Lord was generous to us as His children.

This acute sense of enrichment, pleasure, and well-being has always marked our life beside the sea. The ocean just does that to us. An overwhelming, upwelling stream of gratitude engulfs my entire being for the enormous privilege of being able to live in close company with the ocean. This sensation has never left me. It is as new and fresh and stimulating today as it was thirty-five years ago, when for the first time I actually went to live beside the sea. It was then that the romance blossomed. Nor has my love affair with

the ocean ever diminished a whit. If anything, it has grown ever more virile the more time I spend on the ocean verge.

But those first years by the Straits of Juan de Fuca still stand out as perhaps the most poignant and powerful in my long association with tides, winds, gravel beaches, rocky headlands, and mighty winter storms. I have written elsewhere about those glorious days. My books *Splendour From the Sea, Splendour From the Land,* and *Canada's Wild Glory* describe in detail some of the thrilling events of those adventuresome years. It was then that the ocean cast her spell upon my spirit. It was then the sea became a part of my life. It was then I learned to love her with enormous passion.

I was a young man in my late twenties, determined to own my own piece of land. In vain, for several years, my vivacious bride and I had searched for a spot where we could sink our roots, establish a home, and rear our family in the gentle contentment of a country setting.

One early spring day we followed a rough, winding gravel road that led through the rugged hills on the south coast of Vancouver Island. The narrow road suddenly took a sharp turn, ran out across a beautiful parklike peninsula called Rocky Point, then ended abruptly on a gravel beach. Just offshore stood a picturesque collection of sea-worn rocks and little islands. In the distance beyond towered the impressive peaks of the snow-mantled Olympic Mountains of Washington.

"What a glorious spot!" The expression burst from both of us in unison. It was a seascape of indescribable magnificence. It was so gripping that for a few minutes we could only sit there silently, admiring its native grandeur.

The immediate surroundings had that wild, neglected, uncared-for appearance that creeps over any piece of countryside that once was cultivated, then later abandoned. Ramshackle driftwood shacks, built from bits of driftwood and hand-split cedar shakes, cluttered the beaches. Assorted boats, some half-rotten hulks sinking in the sand with broken bottoms, littered the shore. Old fallen fences, overgrown with wild brambles and tangled roses, ran down to the tide flats.

Yet beyond all of these unsightly intrusions on the scene, a mysterious mood of contentment and tranquility pervaded the place. I began to prowl around the property and found a very old, weathered "For Sale" sign half-buried in the underbrush. Obviously it had been left there years before by some real-estate agent who had given up trying to sell such a derelict spot. For me, it was like stumbling on a vein of high-grade ore. I had found exactly what I wanted. Beneath all the human debris and clutter that defaced the landscape lay a bit of ocean-side land of exquisite beauty.

A few days later I was the delighted owner of 214 acres of abused and beaten land that lay encircled by the sea with over 2 miles of magnificent ocean frontage. That we were still solvent by only 54 cents after paying the full purchase price did not seem to deter our bouyant youthful enthusiasm. We had found our homestead, and we would succeed. Here we would establish ourselves and enjoy a rugged life-style reminiscent of the early pioneers who first settled these shores 100 years before.

The first year or two, our life by the sea was very fragile indeed. More than that, it was

downright precarious. Often it reminded me of the Swiss Family Robinson, who survived merely by their native wit and skill in extracting their sustenance from the ocean world around them.

The very first job was to find some sort of shelter for our little family. We had our first baby girl, and we would need more than a tent for winter weather. We decided to salvage one of the weather-beaten shacks that stood on piles just above high tide. Its roof and walls were patched with fresh cedar shakes I hand split from logs washed up on the shore. A crude crib was fashioned from wave-smoothed boards that we salvaged from the driftwood piles lodged between the sea rocks.

I gathered huge armfuls of fir bark and broken bits of sea-shattered wood to fuel our cast-iron cookstove. The wood was piled in the sun to dry out. Its cost was nothing but the joy of gathering it from the places it had been flung by furious winter gales.

From the gravel bays I hauled enough material to surface a new road that I built to our crude cottage. Every pound of gravel was shoveled by hand. The heavy labor soon gave me the hard muscles and powerful physique of a prizefighter.

We planted a huge fruit and vegetable garden, using our last fifty-four cents to purchase the precious seed for our first crop. I hauled tons of seaweed, clamshells, and kelp fronds onto the tired, worn-out ground for fertilizer. The yields from that patch of revitalized soil were bountiful enough to feed both ourselves and our friends. Baskets of strawberries, raspberries, and currants came off that planting. Buckets and buckets of peas, beans, carrots, potatoes, and other vegetables of a dozen sorts were gathered from that ground. I would work in the long rows of vegetables, stripped to the waist, my body brown as an oak plank, tanned by the sun and cooled by the sea air.

At low tide I took pail, shovel, boots, and lantern to go out in search of the sweet, fat clams that buried themselves among the rocks. My wife's clam chowder and clam cakes became famous far and wide. They were gourmet dishes, equal to the finest served in Victoria's famous Empress Hotel, twenty-five miles across the water.

The coastal black-tailed deer that came down to our beaches to lick the sea salt, nibble the mineral-rich seaweed, and feed on my turnips also helped to fill our larder. More than one fell to my rifle and so was used to supply us with delcious venison stew and delectable venison steaks.

The sea also supplied us with herring and cod and salmon. My Indian neighbors taught me where to fish and how to bait my line. They shared their secrets of the sea with a man whose earlier years had been spent inland, far beyond the mountains. Often, at dusk, when the day's work was done, I would slip out into the straits on a slack tide. Rowing around the offshore island with the sun setting in the west, the only sounds were the quiet dip of my oars, the gurgle of water below the bow of the boat, and the distant sound of sheep bells on my meadows. I doubt, indeed, that there were ever more-sublime moments in any man's life.

As the sun turned red in the west, the silver moon would rise across the sea in the east. In its gentle light, Mount Baker, its snowy crest sheathed in silver, stood stark and beautiful on the skyline. Under such a spell, my little world of velvet—smooth water, a drifting boat, heavy, pungent, fragrant ozone in the air, and salmon splashing—was almost more than a soul could stand.

52/

Then there would be a sudden strike on the line. I was too poor in those distant days to afford a rod, much less a reel. I used only a heavy hand line loaned to me by an ancient mariner. It was wrapped around my bare ankle in the bottom of the boat, while my hard and calloused hands handled the oars. There would be a hefty tug when the salmon struck the bait. The oars would be shipped, and the fish would be played.

It was no small thing to slide one of those thick-bodied beauties into my boat. Its shining silver sides, its powerful tail, its strong streamlined head bespoke a species that is the pride of the Pacific. Its firm, fine-grained, delicious red flesh would feed my family for days and days.

And so, month by month, the sea around us in generous measure gave us shelter, gave us heat, gave us health, gave us meat, gave us strength, gave us heart, and gave us hope. Always the ocean has done this for those who learned to love her and who live beside her.

Over and beyond all of this, the sea along that rock-ribbed coast gave us a joy—a dimension of delight—that is very difficult to put on paper with a pen. It added an element of excitement, stimulation, and also repose that one must experience firsthand to fully understand. As with knowing God, it is not enough to have merely heard about Him; one must come and taste and try and see for oneself how good it can be.

On the hottest summer days, we would slip down to the little gravel bay less than a stone's throw from our cottage door. It was a serene spot. A rich mixture of coast pines, Douglas firs, and western yew trees grew on the rocky bank above the beach. Here was where I beached and tied my boat, which doubled as a crib for our tiny girl, while we stretched out on the shore and took refreshing dips in the cold, crystal-clear water.

The offshore islands sheltered these little coves, so here the sea was most often calm and still and limpid. After a short swim, we would stretch out on the warm stones like contented seals, letting the salt water dry on our suntanned bodies with a delicious tingling sensation. Amid our poverty and privation, we felt enormously rich and sweetly satisfied with life.

What if we did live in a driftwood cottage? What if we did cook on a wood-fired stove? What if we could not afford electric lights or a telephone? What if it was twenty-five miles

to town and its busy streets? What if we had hardly any money? What if we were so short of cash I had to work off my taxes on that gravel road we first followed to find this place beside the sea?

Our lives may have seemed stern and spartan by modern standards. What we may have lacked in cozy comforts or mechanical conveniences, we more than made up for in freedom of spirit and *joie de vivre*. And of all this, the sea was no small part.

We looked out of our spray-spattered windows at a scene which no painter could ever properly portray. The comingled beauty of our own seaside meadows; the wild flowers blooming on the banks; the stunted, wind-twisted trees of Garry oak and pine and fir; the shining silver caps of the roaring riptide that thundered around Race Rocks; the majestic Olympics across the silver Straits of Juan de Fuca; the flights of gulls and grebes and black brant; the movement of wind in the waves and on the grass above high tides, the passing fishing boats that threaded their way between the reefs and rocks—what could ever be paid for such values and views? They were beyond the power of money to buy.

A man does not spend years of life in such a setting and amid such surroundings without some of the ocean's own glory settling down into the very fiber of his own makeup. The sea becomes an integral ingredient in the very warp and woof of one's life. It becomes an inescapable aspect, to which one must and does return, again and again and again.

The call of the sea comes to me even when I am hundreds of miles from its shore. I have stood on the open prairies a thousand miles from the coast and sensed the magnetism of the open ocean. A bittersweet compulsion sweeps over my spirit. Again I yearn for the fragrance of ozone rising from a sun-warmed tide flat. I hanker for the broad expanse of water rippled by the breeze, shining like beaten silver beneath the sun. I long for the great movement of rising tides, with surf breaking on the gray rocks and seabirds on wing crying above the waves.

We had all of these and much, much more on both of the beautiful ranches that I developed by the sea. The first place we called Fair Winds. Five years after we bought it, the government took it from us by expropriation, to use as a naval installation. That such a magnificent site should be selected to store ammunition and armaments is sufficient comment upon the crassness of contemporary society. It is a mark of the utter madness and blind brutality of modern military men.

Our second seaside ranch we called Silver Spray Ranch. Like the first, it too stood on a bold ocean promontory. It was surrounded on two sides by the sea. With over a mile of exquisite oceanfront, it boasted beautiful bays, striking rocky headlands, and gorgeous green meadows that ran down to the very water's edge. Here my children lived in joyous freedom. Here they gathered agates on the beach. Here they plunged in the sea and played their carefree games under sunny skies.

My memories of that spot are of giant seas bursting on the black rocks, in white cascades of foaming water. I can still hear the great roar of their action against the land. I can still feel the tremble and tremor of the earth beneath their impact. I can still see the killer whales surging through those seas. I can be still, even yet, and know, "Oh, God, You made it all! This is Your wondrous world!" /55

Atlantic—Icelanders, Scots and Irish, to name but a few—know that it is the sea which governs their lives. They learn to love the ocean with an intense devotion. The sea around them is the means of their survival. It determines their climate; it provides their livelihood; it conditions their culture, and it fashions the very fabric of their lives.

No one can live for long on an ocean island without it working a certain powerful change in his life-style. It is inevitable that islands condition our human behavior and color our human conduct. Much has been written about the impact of man upon the islands of the sea. Far less has been recorded about the impress of the ocean world upon those who make the islands their home.

It is true that, on the whole, man's record of grievous exploitation and ruination of islands has been a dismal chapter in human history. Over and over, human beings—in ignorance and indifference—have raped and ruined islands of exquisite beauty and fragile loveliness. They have come to these ocean paradises to cut, fell, burn, and clear their virgin forests with crass and cruel carelessness. Some islands have been turned from emerald-green jewels lying in sapphire seas to bare, wind-blown hulks of rock and cinders.

Man's deliberate introduction of his own domestic stock: goats, sheep, cattle, donkeys, hogs, and cats, has led to the ultimate destruction of native vegetation and rare, exotic species of flora and fauna that were unique to their island environment.

The thoughtless importation of foreign birds, rodents, reptiles, and insects from the continental land masses has led to the total extinction of some island species. It is a dark and disastrous story, perpetrated all over the planet. People have been less than fair or reasonable in their exploitation of islands.

The same holds true for the introduction of trees, shrubs, plants, and grasses that often supplanted the island species. For those of us with understanding eyes and knowing hearts, it has been a grim, sad tale. But this book is not primarily about that dark side of the island story. Instead, it is an account of the ocean's glory.

In life, our first impressions of any new environment are often the most enduring. Especially is this so if we are intending to make the new setting our home. All of our senses are keenly alerted. Our spirits and emotions are intensely sensitized. We are fully alive and responsive to our new surroundings. Subconsciously, as well as consciously, we keep asking the questions: "How will I like living here?"—"Does this terrain suit my temperament?"—"Can I really feel comfortable and at ease in this climate and culture?"

All of this was extremely true of me, when, quite late in life, I set out to make a new home in the South Pacific. It then seemed like an enormous adventure for a man in his fiftieth year of life. Already I had behind me half a century of most adventuresome living in various parts of the world. But never before had my zestful spirit or eager enthusiasm been exposed to the restrictions of island living.

Perhaps, like thousands of other people, the romantic aura of the South Seas had cast its spell upon me. I rather doubt this. In sincerity and earnestness, I had read and studied all I could about island life in places as far removed as Hawaii, Fiji, the New Hebrides, and New Zealand. But even with all this foreknowledge, I was not fully prepared for the impact that the South Pacific would make upon my life in the following years.

First of all, it simply must be admitted that ocean islands are breathtakingly beautiful. Even the most glamorous and glossy travel brochures do not really do them justice. Even the photographs reproduced in this book cannot convey the grandeur and glory of island seascapes. There is a depth and dimension of fragile loveliness that eludes the finest photographer and most-perceptive painter. It is something very difficult to define, but it has to do with the tranquility, the tenderness, of the ever-present sea. Such loveliness encompasses and holds to her bosom this child, born and raised from within the depths of her own strong body.

Second, there is the soft, salubrious atmosphere of a maritime climate. Often it is fragrant with the perfume of exotic flowers as pungent as plumeria, golden shower or honeysuckle. It is rich with the aroma of ozone and salt spray.

This is heady stuff. There is no way any of it can be conveyed, either by the photographic chemicals on a film or by the artist's colors on a canvas.

Third, islands have a peculiar remoteness, an austere isolation, a subtle sort of privacy that plays upon the human heart. For some, this is a sweet solace to their spirit. For others, it brings a deep disquiet to their disposition. Not anyone or everyone can become an *islander* indefinitely. For some, the constrictions and cramping and rather rigid restrictions of an island are too confining. They begin to feel a bit trapped—a bit caged. Only those who learn to really love the ocean all around them will feel fully at ease in such a setting.

Speaking for myself, I very soon came to realize that the ocean islands—though a joy to explore and study—would never satisfy me fully as a permanent home. I am a man who

needs and craves mighty mountain ranges. My whole person exults in wide, sweeping plains. I relish the long, lonely vistas of deserts and bush and wild veld. These are the terrain of the great land masses we call continents. They can be found only in rather tiny form on the islands.

Yet, marvel of marvel, they can be found. And it was this discovery, of the great diversity to be found on the ocean islands, that made my years there a beautiful adventure.

I shall never forget the very first trip I made out into the "bush," away from the bright lights and crowded beaches of Honolulu and Waikiki. I made camp in a windswept grove of acacias. They are a species of tree native to my home in Kenya. The soil beneath my boots was the same red laterite of volcanic origin that I had been familiar with as a lad. Stray mongooses skittered through the thorny undergrowth in search of birds, rats, and insects. I might well have been camped in the heart of Kenya's Masai reserve.

Yet, just beyond my camp, the blue Pacific broke on the beach and against the bold bluffs in giant, thundering white breakers. Each comber burst against the rocks like an exploding bomb. Shimmering spray shot into the sky.

I knew without doubt I was on an island; a remote bit of land in the far reaches of a gigantic sea. This tiny cluster of island outposts has no other land neighbor within hundreds and hundreds of empty ocean miles; only surging seas, open skies, and the wind-driven waves lie in unending distances to the east, west, north, and south.

All of this notwithstanding, these Hawaiian Islands are a midocean paradise of exquisite charm. Across the centuries since their fiery birth from beneath the sea, they have been clothed with an ever-changing mantle of vegetation. Some species were borne to the islands by the ocean. They came there carried on the waves, to be washed up and take root on the virgin shore. Others later came with men, first of all in frail seagoing canoes, then in sailing ships, later steamers, and now in swarms of aircraft that arrive daily from every quarter of the globe.

In all of this, there is perpetual change. The Hawaiian Island chain is like an enormous Kew Gardens. Because of the dramatic diversity of its terrain, altitude, and climate, which varies from dry desert to sopping rain forest, almost every species of tree, plant, or grass can grow somewhere here.

Hawaii has sometimes been likened to the Garden of Eden. In more than one way, this is true, for here one sees new species being established in a setting of quiet beauty. Only time will determine those which survive and thrive, those which succumb.

What is true of plant life applies equally to the birds. Strange and exotic species from all over the earth have been introduced to the islands. At first it seems incongruous to see birds from South America, Africa, and Australia side by side. This man-managed invasion has been very detrimental to the native species, some of which teeter on the verge of oblivion. Only a few rare pairs remain entrenched in some of the more remote and inaccessible forests, tucked away in the toughest terrain.

All these impressions sweep over the spirit of anyone sensitive to the splendor and beauty of this ocean world. On every hand, there is constant change—endless flux—the emergence of new life forms.

Standing alone, lost in thought, wonder, and quiet awe, overlooking an island vista, the beautiful passage from Isaiah has often come to my mind.

> Yea, they shall not be planted; yea, they shall not be sown: yea, their stock shall not take root in the earth: and he shall also blow upon them, and they shall wither, and the whirlwind shall take them away as stubble. To whom then will ye liken me, or shall I be equal? saith the Holy One. Lift up your eyes on high, and behold who hath created these things, that bringeth out their host by number: he calleth them all by names by the greatness of his might, for that he is strong in power; not one faileth.
>
> Isaiah 40:24–26

One such interlude especially lingers in my memory. I had climbed carefully to the very summit of the yawning crater of Mount Haleakala on Maui. The lower slopes, as is often the case, had been wrapped in dense veils of mist and fog. As I broke out from beneath these, into the golden sunlight at the summit, I could see the highest points of the other islands, looking like a small flotilla of ships sailing in a sunlit sea.

Completely entranced by the splendor of my surroundings, I strolled quietly about the summit of the barren, desertlike volcano until sundown. Gradually the sun, sinking down toward the ocean to the west, bathed my whole island world in golden radiance. It glistened from the huge expanse of moving sea waves all around. It glanced from the cumulus clouds above the leeward slopes of the island chain. It glowed from the landscape of rocks and trees and meadowlands below, as the mists rolled away. All the earth was alight with an incandescent light—bright and glorious.

It is not often one is so utterly overwhelmed with an outer glory that he finds a response within his spirit, which becomes stilled and silent before the Lord from whom it came. To be there, completely alone on that remote island mountain in midocean at that precise moment of sublime splendor, was an honor of special significance. It was as though I had been allowed to stand briefly within the inner sanctuary of the Most High. It was a humbling hour.

That evening I cared not whether my tongue tasted food or my lips felt the touch of water. I had been nourished and refreshed from a source of inspiration that far transcended any ordinary human comprehension.

To my surprise, when I awoke long before daybreak the next morning, it was to discover a number of young people—all wrapped up in warm blankets and sleeping bags—huddled on the summit rocks. They had come in the night to await the dawn of a new day.

It is in the remote midocean islands that we see firsthand the stern struggle between the sea and land-building forces. It is a ferocious and fearsome process. Nor is it surprising that primitive island people, such as the early Hawaiians, attributed the birth and origin of their world to Pele, the goddess of fire.

I shall never forget the eerie glow cast upwards into the night sky by that gigantic seething furnace of the earth. For miles we could hear the rushing, pulsing, threatening roar of the molten magma rising and falling back into the gaping throat of the volcanic caldera. The somber reminder that came home to my heart in those midnight moments was that men were but a minute moment in the long history of a planet formed by fire.

We were minute creatures, inhabiting the surface of a sphere whose matrix was molten material under enormous pressure, incandescent with heat.

In a comingled attitude of awe and reverence, we picked our way carefully through the fire-lit gloom. From afar we could hear the terrifying turbulence of the earth's inner fires. Suddenly there would be a rushing, thundering roar. A fountain of flowing lava would spill from the depths, to go running over the mountain slope in red rivers of fire. Across the slopes the glowing lava cascaded, in broad bands of lurid orange and livid red. Whatever the lava touched it ignited, so intense was its heat. Grass, shrubs, trees, roots, and rubbish all flamed and smoked and burned before the advancing inferno.

At dawn the next day, Cheri and I tramped across the countryside to observe where the molten lava actually ran over the sea cliffs and tumbled into the Pacific. It was almost as spectacular as the eruptions of the night before.

Gigantic gray-white clouds of steam rose high into the sky all along the shore. The molten magma would run over the rocks behind each succeeding wave. Then, as the next comber came rushing in upon it, there would be the hissing explosion of seawater suddenly superheated and turned to steam. The cooled lava would congeal under the rising clouds of steam, to add a few more feet of solid rock to the island edge.

Across uncounted centuries of time, by erratic stops and starts, mountains rise in this manner from the ocean deep. The colossal pressures of compression within the planet are matched and met by the relentless and remorseless erosion of the sea. Here new land is added and built up by degrees; there it is worn away and cast back into the ocean basins by the battering of 10 billion breakers that roar and thunder against the outer island ramparts.

The end result is the production of some of the earth's most spectacular seascapes. Especially is this true of the windward flanks of any island group or chain. Here the prevailing winds drive the ocean waves against gaunt rock-ribbed bluffs in endlesss torment. The pounding of the surf and the rush of restless waters carve the cliffs into fantastic formations.

This is a realm of perpetual motion and dulling dampness. The surge of the sea, the rising and falling tides, the crash of thousand-ton combers, and the cascading waterfalls from mountainous waves sculpt and shape the stony shore into grim black bays and gaunt gray cliffs.

It is here that limpets and mussels and barnacles cling to the rock faces with fantastic endurance. The sledgehammer blows of the thundering breakers; the rush of titanic tides; the swirling, scouring, sucking action of the angry wind-driven storms cannot tear them loose from their toehold on the stone. Repeatedly, every day, they are soaked and submerged in the sea from which their very life is derived.

All this goes on perpetually along miles of coastline seldom seen by man, seldom visited except by solitary seabirds or the great mammals of the deep. I have hiked for miles and miles along remote coastlines and lonely sea cliffs where not another soul was to be seen. In such places the clamor and clangor of man's civilization is nonexistent. It is a world as primitive, as pristine, as profoundly ancient as that into which the first man ever stepped. It is humbling to walk there alone, with only the sound of the sea around.

It is on these windward coasts that the sea shapes great arches and caves from the crumbling cliffs. The merciless battering of huge, white-maned breakers wears away the softer strata, leaving stark stacks standing in the sea like stern sentinels. In other places yawning sea caves are carved out beneath the bluffs. The inrushing water builds up enormous pressures, which pulverize the softer stone. Eventually a blow hole may be blown clear through the roof of the cavern, creating a vortex through which the sea roars and rages like a giant geyser.

The moaning and groaning of the ocean, as it throbs and pulses through these under-

ground caves and tubes, can be terrifying to the uninitiated. It is as if wild spirits and untamed monsters of the deep dwell in this nether realm. These are the coasts which have so often given rise to fantastic tales of grotesque ocean denizens bent on man's destruction.

To add an even more depressing dimension to these storm-battered headlands, there is their dark, dull weather. As though it were not enough to be under vicious attack from the sea, they are often engulfed with remorseless rain, sleet, snow, or mist. The skies over the windward coasts are often leaden, heavy with cloud, pregnant with downpours of perpetual rain.

These rugged, grim, gaunt ramparts facing the fury of wind and waves are soaked and soaked and soaked. Sea spray, flying spume, breeze-blown brine, mist and fog and sleet and rain all combine to keep the coast eternally drenched and dripping. On some islands in midocean, annual rainfall runs into several hundred inches a year. The sky weeps day after day. The clouds hang low week after week. The sun is blotted from view most of the time. Beneath the bleak, bedeviling overcast, the gray sea surges and swells and storms with leaden heaviness. Looking like molten metal, only its fringes flash white when the wind whips the crest off a wave. It flares silver where its fury is spent in crashing, roaring walls of angry water lashing the ramparts of stone and rock.

In contrast, the leeward sides of ocean islands are often serene, still, sun-drenched strands. The sweeping ocean winds, drained of their moisture on the windward slopes, are balmy and pleasant. They whisper in the fronds of the palms or rustle gently in the tall sea grass.

These are the shores with quiet bays, blue lagoons, rings of coral reefs, sparkling sun-kissed beaches, and bathing beauties. Here is where the tourists, the travelers, the visitors seeking the sun, come in crowds. The weather is generally good; the skies are more often clear than cloudy; the sea is relatively calm; and island life appears to be peaceful and serene.

Surprisingly enough, there are still remote islands here and there, removed from the main air-and-sea-travel routes, where snow-white beaches sparkle in the sun and scarcely a human footprint marks the sand. Cheri and I visited one such island in the New Hebrides. I was sent there on a special assignment to make a land survey. It was like stepping back four thousand years, into a pristine paradise of pure perfection.

We came to a beautiful bay of turquoise blue water. It was almost completely encircled with a ring of picturesque islets. Outside this circle lay coral reefs enclosing multicolored lagoons of aquamarine hues. The beaches were snow-white, formed by the gentle fragmentation of aging coral. They lay shining, resplendent in the sun, overshadowed here and there by the fine filagree of palm fronds waving in the wind.

Wherever we walked, barefooted in our bikinis, we could see no sign of another human footprint on the beach. Shells—all kinds of shells, in magnificent profusion and innumerable designs—littered the shore. There were shells there I had seen only in books before—rare shells, perfect shells, colorful shells. In excitement and glee, we would pick up one, only to put it down a few moments later because it had been superseded by another even more beautiful.

Overhead, gorgeous cumulus clouds drifted across the bright blue skies, like a flotilla of great sailing ships floating on an azure sea. The water was 80° in temperature. After a leisurely swim, we stretched out languidly on the sand. This was a bit of pristine paradise.

Yet, in truth, it must be said that most islands, in their own unique, remarkable manner, have this capacity to capture and excite the interest of us human beings. There is an element of romance, beauty, charm, and adventure attached to any fragment of land that lies out to sea, surrounded by water on every side.

From earliest times, seafaring races have always held a special respect and reverence for islands. It was the ocean isles that provided shelter in the great storms. It was on the islands that early voyagers found fresh water for drinking, fresh food for their crews, and even fresh fuel for their fires. The islands and their offshore reefs and shoals were famous for their fishing grounds. More than all of this, they were new terrain, on which it was possible for hardy adventurers to start new settlements and seek fresh fortunes.

Wherever my travels have taken me, all over the world, this sense of acute excitement has gripped me whenever I have visited an ocean island. It is as if each were a self-

contained little world, packed full of its own special surprises that it willingly shared with anyone who cared enough to take the time to explore it fully.

I shall never forget the very first time in my life this happened. My first bride and I spent our honeymoon on a beautiful island in the Gulf of Georgia. It had glorious beaches of white sand, tiny coves packed with silver-gray driftwood, rocky headlands where the gulls and cormorants nested. Wild flowers flourished in the little fields and sunny woodland clearings along the shore, while a variety of tough native trees, twisted and bent by the fierce sea winds, adorned the shoreline.

It was an exquisite world of sea, land, and sky in which two young lovers roamed, wrapped in wonder, joy, and romance. Day after day, we would set out—barefoot and suntanned—to tramp the tiny, twisting deer trails that ran all over the island. We would carry a thermos of tea, a basket of sandwiches, some fruit, plus a pair of binoculars to study the wildlife. It was a glorious adventure, an interlude in our lives to be treasured forever.

Twenty-five years later, after the painful home-going of my first beloved companion, my second life companion and I did much of our courting on the Hawaiian Islands. Eventually it was there in mid-Pacific that we were married. Our honeymoon was spent within earshot of surf, where the balmy trade winds rustle the palms and the tropical moon turned our island world into beaten silver.

That, too, was an interlude in life that left memories of exquisite delight and delectable joys. Few men indeed have been so favored. In large part, the ecstacy and enjoyment of these intervals were sharpened acutely by the sheer magic and magnetism of their island settings. It is an intoxicating atmosphere that an island can produce, compounded of turquoise seas, great cumulus clouds, trees blowing in the breeze, white surf singing on the beach, warm sands under the sun, birds on wing overhead, the fragrance of flowers in the air, and the loved one lying contentedly in the gentle arms of the lover.

It is not surprising that islands produce a profound upwelling of poignant gratitude to our Father for their romance and native charm. Again and again, there has risen from the depths of my innermost being a tremendous, compelling, irrepressible surge of thanksgiving to God for such beauty, such inspiration, such stimulation of soul and spirit and body as islands can provide. They are a magnificent gift of joy from our Father to His earth children.

Over and over, as constant as the breakers that beat on the beach a few feet from my windows overlooking the sea, there comes to my spirit the magnificent refrains from Psalms 19:1–5:

> The heavens declare the glory of God; and the firmament sheweth his handywork. Day unto day uttereth speech, and night unto night sheweth knowledge. There is no speech nor language, where their voice is not heard. Their line is gone out through all the earth, and their words to the end of the world. In them hath he set a tabernacle for the sun, Which is as a bridegroom coming out of his chamber, and rejoiceth as a strong man to run a race.

Beyond the breakers, across the sun-washed waves, lie a whole chain of islands. Like a pod of great gray whales, their backs arch out of the ocean. On clear days they are a delight to the eye. But beyond this, they beckon to me strongly. Silently but surely, they have already cast their spell upon me. One day soon I shall set sail for their shores. Just the thought of setting foot on a fragment of land I have never trod before stirs me to the depths. It quickens my pulse, arouses my enthusiasm.

Already I have read widely and with excitement about what awaits me on these wind-battered islands. There are high, steep, sharp, formidable cliffs. Here the great brown pelicans, the gulls, and the cormorants nest. When a stranger approaches, they take to the air in flocks, crying loudly at the intrusion.

Here and there, jagged, ragged pinnacles of rock protrude from the ocean depths. They have been battered into startling shapes. Some have been cut away by wind and water, to form arches and coves and stacks of stark stone, strangely beautiful against the blue and white backdrop of the sea and sky.

There are a few small coves and sandy beaches where a boat can shelter briefly. But these same spots are a habitat for harbor seals, sea lions, and other denizens of the deep.

They haul themselves up ponderously from the surf, to stretch out in the sun and sleep unmolested on the sand.

On these islands there is a profusion of wild flowers. Some are rugged and robust, such as the giant Coreopsis, others are frail and fragile, finding shelter in the rocky crevasses away from fierce winds that sometimes lash the islands. On every side there is living evidence that the plant life is in a state of transition. Slowly, native species are returning to an area ravaged by the sheep and rabbits introduced by early island colonists.

But long before the first white settlers, ancient seagoing Indian tribesmen visited these islands in their canoes. Their middens are a mute testimony to the rich fishing grounds that brought them here.

Offshore there are sunken wrecks. Among the reefs and shoals, a prolific array of porpoises, dolphins, fish, and other marine life of a hundred sorts swarm and play in the running tides and currents. Others shelter in the tide pools.

These are all part of the exciting diversity of our ocean islands. Those I see from my windows draw me to come and explore their world. I can no longer resist their pull. It is pure and powerful and persistent. It is a part of the ocean's unique and splendid glory.

I must go!

Our human perspective of the planet may have altered. Our understanding of ocean movements and climatic conditions worldwide may have been tempered by technology. Our compression of distances and time may have made us rather haughty. Still, the ocean's splendor remains.

So it is that a person—you, the reader of these pages, or anyone else who wishes to understand the greatness of the sea—must spend time with it. As with mountains, it is not enough to merely traverse them in some high-speed machine. Nor will it do to just view them from a rather remote and detached viewpoint. One simply has to come into intimate and personal contact to fully develop any sort of genuine respect for the enormous power and prestige of the sea.

I believe this is why books written by brave men and women who have sailed the seas, especially in small craft, have always captured the attention of the public. Heroic individuals—whether in very ancient and primitive craft such as wooden canoes, reed boats, log rafts, ox-hide caravels, or sailing ships—setting out to explore the oceans, have always aroused great excitement, not only because they were so brave in risking their lives, but also because of the enormous expanse of the oceans on which they embarked. It was essentially a contest between the spirit of adventure in man and the mighty forces of the often-unknown seas.

Even down to the closing years of this twentieth century, the exploits of hardy individuals challenging the mighty seas in small craft, often almost single-handedly, thrill us to the depths. Take, for instance, the great adventures of the *Dove,* sailed by a teenage lad from California clear around the world; or the equally exciting exploits of that ancient mariner Sir Francis Chichester, who, late in the twilight of his life, circumnavigated the globe in record time, single-handed, in his swift sloop *Gypsy Moth.*

In the same category, we have to place people like Thor Heyerdahl, who with a very tiny crew set sail across the earth's mightiest oceans in crude craft of primitive design. Drifting on a raft of logs such as the *Kon-Tiki,* he crossed the South Pacific. Similarly, he set sail across the Atlantic in a boat built from bundles of bulrushes and reeds.

All such men—and there have been a host of them—who for prolonged periods lived in private, personal, intimate contact with the ocean, speak of it with intense love and a compelling respect. For some, their periods at sea have been painful, dreadfully dangerous, thrilling, challenging, yet deeply rewarding. Oceans just do that to people, drawing them back again and again.

There are some aspects of the ocean that twentieth-century technology has opened up to our understanding with tremendous interest. One of these great discoveries is that all the water of all the oceans is in fact one gigantic fluid. It is in constant motion and movement, circulating by means of colossal currents from pole to pole and clear around the earth.

The ancient idea that each ocean or great inland sea, such as the Mediterranean, was more or less a self-contained body of water, restricted roughly within its own continental basin and boundaries, is no longer valid. We know now for a fact that these great oceans actually flow into one another in gigantic subsurface rivers that make the Mississippi, Nile, or Amazon seem like mere trickles in comparison. The water that one year is torn

and tossed in a tropical typhoon at the equator may at a later date be locked in clear-blue ice within the Arctic Circle.

The Mediterranean Sea, that beautiful body of water of exquisite blue, if not recharged by the great gray Atlantic, would gradually dry up. The actual rate of evaporation from the Mediterranean exceeds the volume of fresh water that pours into it from the various rivers and streams of Europe and North Africa. But through the Straits of Gibraltar there flows an enormous and powerful current of saline seawater to compensate for the daily loss. In olden times, before the advent of power-driven ships, mariners would have to wait for days and days to catch exactly the right sea conditions that would carry them out through the Straits of Gibraltar to the open Atlantic beyond.

Some of these ocean currents move with remarkable regularity and precision. A small inkling of their formidable force and fantastic flow can be grasped when they come into conflict with a rising or falling tide. My very first home by the sea was on the southernmost extremity of Vancouver Island. Here a rocky peninsula, well named Rocky Point, jutted out like a gnarled clenched fist into the famous Straits of Juan de Fuca. Just offshore stood a small, weather-beaten, storm-lashed outcrop of black rocks, well-known as Race Rocks. On this gale-lashed collection of stone stood a great lighthouse. Between it and us was the race.

Here the tides roared and surged and thundered. In raging whitecaps and angry seas, the current and tides were in conflict. Even on a dead-calm summer day, we could see and hear the foaming, frothing walls of water, churned up without any wind or storm, straining against one another.

All the local fishermen and tugboat captains knew about the race. They planned their passages around the point to take advantage of the best tides and times, knowing full well it was folly to try to force a passage when the sea was making up and a rip was on.

Often I would stand alone and silent, lost in wonder at the overwhelming power of the ocean currents that surged in and out of the straits. In fact I came to respect them with a deep and profound reverence. They had caused many a shipwreck and taken many a life.

One of these was of a dear, brave friend. He had come to live on the island after World War II. Andy was a lighthearted, joyous, carefree cockney from the heart of London. During the war he had been a jaunty, daring airman, who flew innumerable sorties over enemy territory. He was not a man given to fear.

He and his wife and little family eventually became the lighthouse keepers on Race Rocks. Between tides, he would tear across the race in his tiny cockleshell of a boat to retrieve mail, groceries, and whatever spartan supplies were needed for his family's rigorous life on the rocks. Often he would stop in at our wee cottage for a "spot of tea" and a bit of lighthearted banter.

One Christmas he came across in blustery weather. For more than a week, he had waited impatiently for the sea to settle. At last he would wait no longer. Taking his life in his hands, he decided to make a run for it. He did not wish to disappoint his wife and children over Christmas. There would be packets of mail, Christmas parcels, a turkey, yes, even a Christmas tree that I had cut especially for him and his family.

As we loaded the supplies into his little boat, I begged him to wait a bit. I could hear the race raging. Through the December grayness and gloom, I could see the whiteness of the roaring rip.

I begged him to sleep at our place. Perhaps the next day the straits would calm down a little. But Andy was set to go. Nothing would deter him. He had faced rough waters before. With a jaunty wave of his frayed seaman's cap, he turned his boat into the tide. The little Christmas tree bobbed away at the bow. His motor roared and he was away, off into the rip.

It was the last time anyone ever saw Andy. Out on the lonely light, his wife stared and strained her eyes to get even a glimpse of a small white boat that never came. A wee girl wept and pleaded for her daddy, who vanished forever. For days, I and my neighbors tramped the shores and beaches of our seagirt world, but no sign of Andy's body was ever found. Weeks later, his battered boat washed up on a remote beach on the Washington coast. It had been carried miles and miles to sea by the vagaries of ocean tides and currents, which no man could ever tame or control.

Only those of us who have lived in close and intimate contact with these mighty ocean currents fully appreciate their remorseless power and tumultuous energy. Day and night, year after year, it is expended all around the earth; yet, strange to say, scarcely any of it has ever been harnessed or turned to useful purposes.

Often, as I have stood watching the breakers burst in white foam along miles of beach, the question has come to me: "Why has not some of this energy been harnessed?" It seems almost incongruous that scientific technology of the twentieth century has virtually left untouched the stupendous store of energy exerted by ocean tides and currents.

/81

The eternal, inexorable movement of literally trillions of tons of water every day of the year represents an expenditure of energy that dwarfs man's most-sophisticated schemes.

It matters not whether we contemplate the might and magnificence of the magnetic and gravitational forces that oscillate the oceans on a worldwide scale, or whether we see but a single small segment of this energy expended in one spot in one fierce rip; on every hand, there is overwhelming power present.

This power, of which we are aware, humbles our haughtiness. It sobers our spirits. It exalts our souls in quiet reverence. For me, as a man, it bids me bow myself in wonder. "Oh, my Father—this is Your world. You made it. You sustain it!"

In such interludes of contemplation, there sweeps into my remembrance those inspired lines from the Scriptures:

> Now Christ is the visible expression of the invisible God. He was born before creation began, for it was through him that everything was made, whether heavenly or earthly, seen or unseen. Through him, and for him, also, were created power and dominion, ownership and authority. In fact, all things were created through, and for, him. He is both the first principle and the upholding principle of the whole scheme of creation.
> Colossians 1:15–17 PHILLIPS

We recognize that, amid the raging of gigantic ocean storms and movements of the sea, there is eternal change. We see coasts cut away and sculpted by relentless erosion.

84/

Land masses shift and buckle, to form enormous oceanic canyons or submarine mountains. Gigantic ocean currents, flowing thousands of miles, change their courses, alter climates, and bring life or death to continental littorals. Arctic and Antarctic ice caps freeze and thaw, expand and contract. Oceans rise in some periods of history, fall in others. Gigantic inland seas subside, to leave behind vast coastal plains. At other times the ocean returns, to inundate the land and bury immense land masses beneath its briny waves.

All of this has been going on for eons. The record is written clearly in the fossil remains of rocks now forming high mountain ranges. I have come across perfect specimens of seashells in limestone ridges at 10,000 feet elevation on the crest of the Canadian Rockies. Likewise I have flown across great wastes of the Sahara Desert, where, etched clearly in the desert sand, are the ocean deposits of a once-gigantic inland sea. Wave upon wave, dune upon dune of sea-formed sand stretches across the landscape as an incredible display of the ocean's relentless impact upon the planet.

None of this has happened in wild disorder. All of these changes occur under physical and biological laws of meticulous order and precision. There is on every side unmistakable evidence of divine design and supernatural programming. The elemental forces at work shaping the planet, moving the oceans, controlling the climate, determining the survival or extinction of species, are not random influences. They have been planned with precision. They have been programmed with meticulous attention to detail. They are proceeding in proper order, not by blind chance.

The ocean reminds me of this in its own majestic movements.

The incredible splendor of the sea, which lies beyond most of us, is its control of the earth's climate. Very few people, especially those living inland, realize its influence on their everyday affairs. Weather is the most widely discussed subject in all the world, yet its pattern of behavior from week to week is the majestic work of the earth's oceans.

In the northern hemisphere, roughly 61 percent of the globe's surface is under water; in the southern hemisphere, about 81 percent. This gigantic preponderance of ocean coverage determines, to a very large degree, what weather prevails at any given place at any given season.

The reason for this is the amazing and very remarkable chemical and physical qualities of seawater. In all of the universe, there really is no other commodity to compare with it; yet on planet earth, it is our most ubiquitous material. As so often happens, we discover the divine in the very ordinary.

First and foremost, it is astonishing to realize that one cubic mile of ocean water has the capacity to absorb and retain 3000 times as much heat as an equal quantity of air. In layman's language, using contemporary terminology, we can say that roughly 72 percent of the earth's surface is covered with a colossal mantle of heat-absorbing material in fluid form. There is no other sphere in space, to our knowledge, so cloaked in a mantle of water that absorbs solar radiation to modify and temper its total climate.

By virtue of the ocean's incredible capacity to hold the sun's heat, it is in turn capable

of warming the envelope of air that lies above it. For, in fact, there are two oceans that lie contiguous to each other, interacting upon each other, creating the gigantic air and sea currents of the world. The one is the heaving, oscillating, flowing ocean of water; the other is the wide, wild, boisterous, blowing ocean of air lying above it.

The enormous quantities of solar heat and energy absorbed by the ocean of seawater through insolation (warming by the sun) is gently, quietly, and continuously released back into the atmosphere (ocean of air), forming high- and low-pressure systems.

When we pause to remember that one cubic mile of ocean, in cooling down only 1° F, discharges into the air above it sufficient heat to warm 3,000 cubic miles of atmosphere 1° F, we are awestruck. This is why, as the earth turns upon its axis every twenty-four hours, the difference between night and day is sufficiently temperate to allow life to flourish. Were it not for the thermostatic influence of oceans, the shaded side of earth would be gripped in deadly cold, and the sunward side consumed in fierce heat.

Of course we must also remember that, to a much lesser and insignificant degree, there are times when the winds (air currents in motion) moving across the sea can cool or warm its surface. This influence really is of much less consequence at any given time and place. The basic fact remains that it is the sea itself which dominates and determines to a larger degree what the wind systems will be that blow above it. Its meteorological impact, combined with the spinning of the planet upon its own axis, give rise to the predominant wind patterns that prevail across the globe.

Just as there are gigantic wind systems that encircle the earth in its ocean of air, so likewise there are huge sea currents of warm and cold water that circulate throughout the ocean of water. All of these interact in accordance with very definite physical laws and principles. Nor are these fundamental forces the product of blind chance. They function in wondrous order. They operate with splendid precision. They are beautifully balanced. They are programmed to proceed in such a manner that life upon the planet is not only possible, but also preserved in ongoing proliferation.

By this I do not only refer to the thousands of unique forms of marine life that are found in the ocean. I also refer to the incredible array of life that has adapted itself to the land masses. It is from the sea that any moisture must originally come that will fall upon the soil of the continents and islands as rain. It is from the sea that water is evaporated into the atmosphere to form clouds.

All over the oceans, worldwide, there is the restless, never-ending, gigantic spawning of weather systems. Huge cloud formations arise, towering thousands of feet into the wide skies. Their proportions dwarf the earth's mightiest mountain ranges. In a single tropical storm, ten billion tons of water will be evaporated from the ocean surface, to rise forty thousand feet into the atmosphere. Driven and propelled under its own physical forces, it will sweep a thousand miles across the ocean, to unload its burden of moisture on some parched land mass.

The ancient seers, writing under the inspiration of God's own Spirit, were aware of such phenomena long before the basic principles of physics and chemistry had begun to be unraveled by man:

> God thundereth marvellously with his voice; great things doeth he, which we cannot comprehend. For he saith to the snow, Be thou on the earth; likewise to the small rain, and to the great rain of his strength.
>
> Job 37:5, 6

Year in, year out, inexorably across the centuries, the ocean—in all of its unmatched glory and splendor—saturates the earth's atmosphere with moisture. It is the formation of these breathtakingly beautiful cloud patterns enveloping the earth that also helps to make life as pleasant as it is. The cloud layer in the earth's atmosphere helps to shield it from excessive solar radiation. It prevents undue desiccation on the surface of warm land. It gives rise to the glorious beauty of our skies. It plays a prominent part in the incredible loveliness of sunrises and sunsets that turn sea and earth to molten gold. It is the veil of exquisite whiteness that is drawn delicately across the face of the earth, causing us to gasp in ecstatic awe when we fly above it.

If we are people sensitive in spirit to the splendor of our world, such phenomena make us pause to give thanks to our Father. Scarcely a day passes that alone, lost in awe, I do not raise my eyes to the skies and give gratitude to God for winds and rain and clouds and waves and sunrises and sunsets. They are the weather workshop of the world—my world—my Father's world.

From my home on the beach, I watch the weather every day. I see the ocean clouds

the farthest horizon. Slowly but surely, the thunderheads
...rcle of the earth at the extremity of my vision. From my
...first only as a thin white line of undulating cloud, barely
...horizon line. As the day progresses and moisture evaporates
...uds rise higher and higher. Giant cumulus formations climb,
...heavens.

...e landward, drawn in by the low-pressure areas lying over the
...wly and sedately, like huge ships under full sail, the billowing
...proach the offshore islands. As they do, dark ribbons of moisture
...om their edges, like water flowing from a ship's scuppers. Steadily
...d, pushed by the great sea winds that now lift them into towering,
...reaching tremendous heights.

I am... man, a mite, standing on the shore watching a panorama of great glory
unfold. The very tops and summits of the cloud masses catch the sunlight. It is reflected
from their pinnacles in silver, rose, and golden light that radiates off across the sea. At
times it is like a full-orbed sunset coming from due south, turning the ocean waves to
purple, mauve, and orchid hues.

In a few more moments, the moving storm touches the coast. The powerful sea winds
push the mountains of cloud across the mountains of rock. The compressed, moisture-
laden air begins to darken the sky. The clouds grow black, ominous, threatening. Thunder roars. Lightning flashes. Rain begins to fall. And soon the earth is moist, damp, and
fragrant with moisture. It has been refreshed with raindrops that earlier were the ocean
brine flowing through the gills of a swordfish in the far reaches of the Pacific.

The storm passes. The land lies quiescent. Moisture drips from leaves and twigs. Birds
warble contentedly in the trees. A multicolored rainbow arches over the hills in a final
farewell. Yes, all is well.

The ocean has refreshed the earth.

The ocean has refreshed a man.

This is part of the ocean's glory—and hers alone.

Besides the spectacular storms that are such a dramatic part of any seascape, there are
also the wide skies, with their glorious sunrises and sunsets. Those who live along the
ocean verge or on islands, or travel by ship, are enormously impressed with the ever-
changing panorama of their seagirt world.

The ocean has many moods. It is by no means a dull, boring environment. Under
sunlight, fog, mist, rain, broken clouds, and glinting moonlight, its character changes
from hour to hour. There is an element of both romance and raw power in the ocean. It
commands our respect yet allures us with its own extraordinary charm. Even in the face
of raging seas and howling winds, there persists a peculiar hate-love relationship. It is
difficult to define, too elusive to explain precisely.

My own conviction is that the ocean calls loudly to anyone who may feel cramped or
restricted by crowded conditions on land. Its great open spaces, its wide vistas stretching to eternity, its uncluttered sweep of wind-stirred surfaces, its enormous skies vault-
ing from horizon to horizon, give the sense of freedom comingled with solitude many of
us crave vehemently.

Just yesterday I watched a young man and a young lady, obviously very much in love with life, with each other, and with the sea, gamboling on the seashore. A strong westerly wind was gusting up the beach. It stirred up the sea into racing whitecaps. It bent the palms with its pressure. It swept the sand before it in long, trailing eddies. The two young people, hair flying, faces radiant with smiles, leaped and danced and skipped along the shore. They were playing in the sharp sea wind. It tingled their faces; it exhilarated their spirits; it enlivened every fiber of their youthful figures.

This is part of the contagion of the sea.

It is a measure of its magic.

It is part of its attraction.

It is its joy.

Beyond all of this, it provides a place where a man or woman can pause quietly to think deep thoughts. It affords the solitude a soul needs to come apart from the pressures of life and meditate awhile. It supplies the inspiration so essential to man's spirit if he is to retain his self-respect, seeing himself as a child of God.

The sea is a tonic for tension.

The waves bring healing.

The ocean breezes speak peace.

All of this is possible because of the "aliveness" of the sea. It is not a static mass of water contained in giant ocean basins; it is moving, dynamic, vibrant, with colossal currents at work within its mass.

Perhaps the most famous of these is the well-known Gulf Stream of the North Atlantic. This is, in reality, a gigantic river of warm tropical water that originates in the sunny

Caribbean. Having picked up and stored enormous quantities of solar heat from the equatorial region, it steadily moves northward, along the eastern seaboard of the United States.

It is a titanic oceanic current that streams relentlessly toward the arctic, despite encountering the southward flow of the chill Labrador Current. This cold current carries with it huge icebergs and ice floes that have broken away from the grim, gaunt shores of the polar seas. Yet it cannot cancel out the effect of the giant Gulf Stream, for its waters are being steadily replenished with a huge inflow of warm water from the West Indies.

As the Gulf Stream flows offshore, it creates low-pressure weather systems over its surface. These draw in powerful winds of cold air from across the continent and northern Canada. If the general average temperature of the Gulf Stream current increases even a few degrees, it can produce severe winter weather all along the eastern seaboard. Intense storms, with heavy snow, sleet, and freezing rain will sweep in from the continent toward the low-pressure systems at sea.

Steadily, the Gulf Stream pressures its course into the far reaches of the North Atlantic, where it begins to divide and branch. A part of it pushes along the coast of Greenland. Some of it flows eastward, toward Iceland and Spitsbergen. The greater part circulates slowly around the British Isles, along the coast of France, and back down toward Spain and Portugal.

Some of this warm equatorial water will have traveled four or five thousand miles through the ocean. Its presence produces some of the highest sea temperatures found

anywhere in the world at such extreme latitudes. Its impact on the climate of Europe is enormous.

Warm rains and balmy breezes blow across Ireland, England, France, Holland, and most of western Europe. Fields are green. Farms flourish. Livestock can spend the winters outdoors. Frost and ice and snow are more of a rarity than the rule. Springs come early. Birds abound. Planting of crops can commence long before those places not blessed by the Gulf Stream's presence.

If, because of upheavals in the storm patterns in the North Atlantic, the Gulf Stream current is in any way diminished or diverted, the consequences for continental Europe can be catastrophic. Britain, France, and northern Europe are buried under snow. Sleet and ice paralyze the countryside. People suffer agony from the chill weather in their poorly heated homes, and all of life becomes an ordeal until the welcome return of the warm ocean currents.

Similar effects can be found all over the earth. Only the constant, uniform flow of ocean currents insures the stability of climatic conditions in any given place at any given time. Far less is known about these great water movements than we care to either admit or acknowledge. It is a study which will increasingly occupy the attention of oceanographers in the years to come.

For me, however, as a lay person, it is awesome to realize that in part this, too, is a portion of the ocean's great glory. Irresistible, unharnessed, untamed, primitive in her power, she controls, in large measure, the climatic conditions of all the earth.

94/

Hast thou entered
into the treasures of the snow?
or hast thou seen the treasures of
the hail, Which I have
reserved against the time of trouble,
against the day of battle and war?
By what way is the light parted, which
scattereth the east wind upon the earth?
Who hath divided a watercourse
for the overflowing of waters,
or a way for the lightning of thunder;
To cause it to rain on the earth,
where no man is; on the wilderness,
wherein there is no man; To satisfy
the desolate and waste ground;
and to cause the bud
of the tender herb to spring forth?
Hath the rain a father?
or who hath begotten the drops of dew?

Job 38:22 – 28

5

Tide-Line Treasures and Rich Deposits of the Deep

For the vast majority of us who love the ocean and spend time in her company, there are two realms we recognize readily. The first, and by far most conspicuous, is that of the sea edge and surface waters. The other is the enormous ocean depths—a region which represents the last great frontier on earth.

To a greater or lesser degree, most of us are familiar with the tide line. For the great majority of mankind, the giant deeps remain an unknown world—dark, cold, forbidding. Its frontiers have been breached by a few fearless explorers, who have brought back exciting photographs and remarkable accounts of their discoveries.

Most of us, however, are content to stroll quietly along the tide line, learning what we can from the treasures tossed up there by the restless waves. The tidal zone lying between extreme high tide and extreme low tide is one of the most stimulating and exciting in all the world. It is never exactly the same any two days in a row. It is eternally subject to change and modification, depending upon the action and temper of the ocean.

This continuous drama, which proceeds without letup—hour after hour, day after day, week after week, month upon month, year upon year, century upon century, down across eons of time—has always fascinated man. Because it is directly linked to and interlocked with the movement of other spheres in outer space, it grips our imaginations and stirs our spirits.

Our own few years on earth are so brief, so few, so fleeting, so fragile. Like the patterns shaped in sand by wind and tide, they are here for but an hour today, then gone tomorrow. The ebb and flow of the sea across the shore is as changeful as the ebb and flow of humankind across the pages of history.

So if we are essentially men of integrity, we must ask the ancient questions that have always come to the questing heart: "Why am I here? Where did I come from? Where do I go when it is over?"

Are there any lessons to be learned at the tide line? Are there treasures tossed up on the beach that can help to unlock the great mysteries of life? For those who come there to meditate quietly in spirit, open and receptive to the message of the sea, the answer is yes. I say this without embarrassment or apology. The ocean can speak reassuringly. It can carry distinct, definite, detailed impressions to those who spend time there in openness of spirit and humility of heart.

As with the ancient poet, we must cry from the depths of our being: "When I consider thy heavens, the work of thy fingers, the moon and the stars, which thou hast ordained; What is man, that thou art mindful of him? and the son of man, that thou visitest him?" (Psalms 8:3, 4.)

My little life and your little life are not for nothing. Our short stay upon the shores of time is not a mockery. We are not here today, gone tomorrow because of blind fate or the whimsy of fickle fortune. Just as each grain of wave-washed sand; each stone, smoothed and rounded by the sea; each stick of silvered driftwood; each fragment of fragile flotsam; each shell shining in the sun contributes something of beauty and something of value to the passing scene, so likewise can my life and yours.

We are not here merely to serve our own little self-centered ends. I am not a cocky cockleshell, lying smugly on the sands of time, content to conclude that because I contain a thimbleful of seawater I hold the whole ocean in my embrace. Somehow I must see that, though I cradle a tiny part of the whole cosmos in my being, the entire cosmos in turn enfolds me within its embrace. Something of the gracious Spirit of God, my Father, does indeed deign to dwell within my spirit. But by the same token, I live and move and

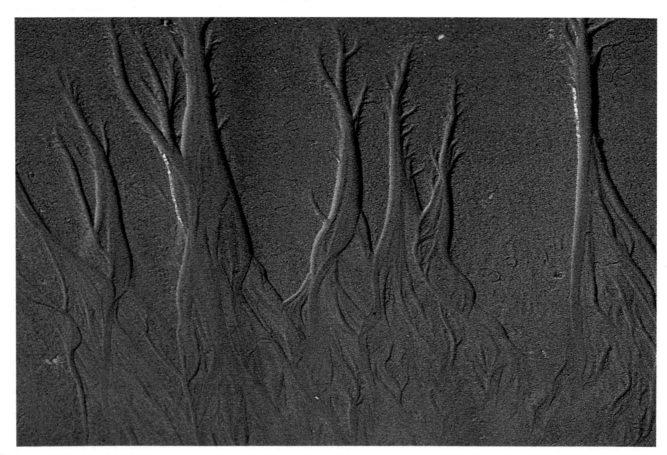

have my very being in Him whose presence and Spirit surround me on every side.

Often, alone and unobserved by any other human being, I walk beside the sea, lost in wonder, hope, and joy. From out of my innermost depths in unrestrained awe and gratitude, there wells up an overwhelming stream of praise for the presence of my gracious Lord. "Oh, my Father, not only are You within my very spirit, by Your Spirit, but also You are without, surrounding me on every side. It is under the never-ending, never-tiring, never-changing impulse of Your presence that I am privileged to move amid a realm of such extraordinary and exquisite beauty, power, and diversity."

It is not that I am detached from, nor a stranger to, the seashore. It is not that I am an objective observer apart from the scene. It is not that I am a stranger standing on the sidelines, watching life go by me. Life simply is not of that sort. It is not that simple. It is not that mechanical. The instant I stand on the beach, I become a part of the scene. The interludes shared with the shore immediately make an impact upon me. My passing feet leave footprints on the soft sand. The passing impressions of my moments by the ocean similarly leave their mark upon my memory and character.

I, as a person, am the sum total of not only all the choices and decisions of my days, but also the final product of all the molding, shaping influences that have played upon me from before birth. Whether I recognized them or not, these have been God-ordained elements of beauty and divinely ordered systems of exquisite artistry surrounding me on every side. Were it not so, most men would be brutes. Even in our ignorance and dullness and indifference, the gracious, gentle, good, and wondrous influence of our natural surroundings ennobles us to a degree.

Evidence of this can be seen in the fact that all that is fine and beautiful in our arts and crafts springs from the source of natural inspiration around us. And of this, the sea and tidelands are no small part.

The flight of seabirds on wing; the fluid lines of fish swimming; the gentle arcs of clouds crossing the sky; the rolling action of waves breaking on a beach; the grandeur of gaunt granite cliffs; the flowing of streams and rivers into the ocean; the smooth lines of wave-worn driftwood; the bending and bowing of grass and trees beneath the wind; the graceful curls and whorls of seashells and marine life; the feathery fronds of ocean plants—all have played a prominent role in human art, music, literature, and culture.

Unconsciously, whether we wish to admit it or not, the sea has shaped and molded the minds, emotions, and instincts of our race. There have been treasures of the tide line that have naturally found a place of value and esteem in our culture and in our traditions. Nor is this something that has had to be learned by rote or ritual. Each new generation discovers with delight the peculiar power possessed by the ocean to elicit our love and admiration.

Just yesterday, my wife and I visited a secluded stretch of shoreline known to very few people. It is an unusually pretty spot, lying at the base of warm brown cliffs, hidden from view by a screen of trees and wild land grown up in brush and weeds.

We were not alone on the beach. Several other couples were also exploring its rock outcrops, its stretches of sand, its coves and reefs, and its wave-sculpted stones. What deeply impressed me was that each person, in his own personal, private, profound way,

had found treasure at this tide line. They were richer in various ways for having been there. The ocean was making its mark upon them: perhaps not something spectacular or dramatic, but nevertheless enduring and beautiful.

One young man, bronzed by the sun, with long golden locks and a vigorous, strongly muscled body, was bearing great pieces of driftwood up the steep path. He was terribly excited about the treasure trove of wood that he was lashing to the top of his ancient car. He made trip after trip up and down the hill, reveling in the adventure of finding free fuel for his fireplace. When it flamed in his hearth, it would bring back again the joy and excitement of these hours beside the sea.

Another young couple, alive and charged with the enthusiasm of youth, romped and splashed in the waves. The salt water tingled on their skin. It flashed silver in sparkling spray as they tossed it from their hair. Every movment they made was charged with gaiety, fun, and joyous well-being. There was health, zest, and vigor to be found between the tides.

My wife, Cheri (her pet name), reveled in our newfound hidden cove. She stretched herself, relaxed her lovely form, and enjoyed the sweet seclusion of our seagirt world. Attired in her shell-white bikini, she bared herself to the spring sun like a contented seal luxuriating on the smooth sand. The sea breeze played in her golden hair, and the sweet aroma of the shore brought a happy smile to her lips. For a few lazy, golden hours, she treasured up the sweet tranquility of the tide line.

As she went to sleep in the sun, I strolled between the tide lines, open and receptive to any message that they might have. I gathered shells. Each has its own private history. There is a peculiar fascination in finding shells. Each has been tossed up between the

tide lines by waves and wind. Each lies there as a reminder of the rich animal life present in the sea. But beyond this is their beauty of form, delicacy of design, and richness of color. Just one perfect shell makes an afternoon by the sea complete. We go away richer than when we came.

This is not because there is any inherent commercial value in the shell itself, although some collectors do have very rare and valuable specimens in their possession. But more often the intrinsic worth of the shell lies in what it represents. It is a symbol, a reminder, a tiny memento of special moments when the ocean's glory, the ocean's character, made its own special mark upon my soul and spirit.

In our home there is a tiny handwoven basket made from grass. It was fashioned by the skillful hands of a very primitive seafaring race of aboriginal Japanese fishermen. In it, Cheri and I have placed the most precious and beautiful of the seashells we have collected in our wanderings around the world. There are special specimens: from Canada's North Pacific coast; from Mexico's desert beaches; from Hawaii's outer islands; from Fiji; from New Zealand's lonely, lovely bays; from Australia's great tide-swept sands; from tropical lagoons in the New Hebrides; and from our beloved California coast.

The strange thing is, we don't just save these shells for ourselves. Again and again, the little grass basket is opened. Its contents are tumbled out on a table. Children especially are invited to enjoy the shining horde. They are encouraged to choose one or two that especially catch their eyes and fancies. These they take home, clutched tightly in tiny

/103

fists or tucked away securely in a little pocket. The shells are shared. Our treasure trove from between the tides has been scattered to a score of homes. Yet somehow the supply never diminishes, never is totally depleted, for it is constantly being replenished from the sea we love so much; the sea that shares its bounty with us.

Precisely the same principle applies to stones, driftwood, coral, and other sea treasures tossed up on the beach by rising tides and raging storms.

My personal penchant is driftwood. It is a strange yet remarkable fact that chunks of root, twisted tree branches, broken bark, and bits of sand-smoothed wood enrich my days beyond my ability to explain.

Partly, of course, it is because of my intense love for the outdoors. Partly it is because of my deep distaste for anything artificial. Partly it is because of the rare beauty brought forth from very rough, ordinary material in a most natural way. Partly it is because of the endless variety and unique character of each piece that has been shaped, scoured, smoothed, and polished by sand and water. No man's hand has had a part in the performance. It comes to me as a special treasure, straight from the workshop of the sea.

Since I first lived by the sea, there have always been lovely pieces of driftwood in my home. Some of them were so tiny they would almost fit in a lady's thimble. Others have been so majestic and massive they well-nigh dominated the living room. Like the seashells, there is nothing staid or static about these treasures that I have hauled home in my hip pocket or in the trunk of my car.

They come and they go. Sometimes they share our home for only a few hours, other times for several years. But sooner or later a friend falls in love with one of the pieces, and away it goes, to gladden another heart and cheer another home. Pieces of my driftwood can be found in scores of homes all over the world. Part of their greatest worth is the joy of sharing them with someone else.

What is true of shells and driftwood is likewise true of stones and rocks, of unusual character and beauty, gathered from bays and beaches all over the world. In our humble cottage home there stands a glass jar of water, filled with beautiful shiny stones that have come from far-off ocean shores.

Looking at those stones, I am reminded again and again of the ocean's glory on a distant strand that my feet have trod. Some have been quiet places under gentle tides and warm winds. Others were gathered from rock-girt bays, where white water thundered against the land.

Depending on their origin, the stones come in all colors, from snow-white to jet black. All of them are smooth to the touch, polished to exquisite perfection, having been tumbled in the wash of the waves for uncounted years.

One gorgeous shell-white cluster of stones, formed from pure quartz on a remote and lonely New Zealand beach, I had made into a set of earrings and a pendant for Cheri. Their soft glow and symmetrical beauty needed no further finishing by man's methods or machines. They possess a special natural charm all their own.

There are innumerable little gravel beaches on some coasts that are formed entirely of small smooth stones. Here one can pick up agates and other semiprecious stones of a hundred sorts. Each tiny stone has behind it an incredible history of development. It

may originally have been a part of some majestic mountain, far inland. Through weathering, fragmentation, glaciation, and the rumbling mills of a racing river, the stone was steadily shaped and borne seaward by the earth's forces of erosion. Finally it would be flung out upon some far shore, to be ground and tumbled in the rise and fall of ten thousand tides.

This is the way in which many beaches in northern latitudes have been built from the basic bedrock of the earth. The wearing away of cliffs, the erosion of river and stream estuaries, the grinding mills of heavy surf and pounding waves reduce rock to smaller rounded stones, which gradually wear away to sand and silt.

Most of us are not consciously aware of the colossal cycle of moving waters: rising from the ocean in steady evaporation; borne landward by the winds; falling in the form of mist, rain, snow, and sleet; then flowing back again into the sea by way of innumerable streams, rivers, and subterranean springs of fresh water. This is one of the most critical and complex of all cycles in the ecosystem. If it failed to function, even for a few short weeks, all life on land surfaces would soon begin to deteriorate and perish.

A part of the ocean's glory is the fact that it is the main repository of the earth's life-sustaining moisture. From the giant ocean basins, moving wind systems, bearing huge cloud formations, transport billions of tons of water to the thirsty land and parched soil of all the continents and islands. There it falls to the ground in various forms. In some places it comes as softly as veils of mist and shrouds of fog. In other areas it may descend in flurries of snow or windblown sleet. In the warmer climes, it may pour down in torrential typhoons or massive monsoons that dump several inches of water on the earth in a few short hours.

This moisture falling upon the land refreshes vegetation, fosters new growth, provides the means for physiological processes to proceed, sustains plant and animal life, and determines what species shall and can survive in any given situation or locale. To a large extent, it determines climate and decrees what weather shall prevail upon the land. It conditions and controls the productivity of forests, fields, grasslands, and semidesert regions.

Whether or not man cares to recognize and acknowledge this majestic role of the ocean in his own survival is really beside the point. The fact remains that it is so. Ultimately, his own welfare is linked directly to the ocean. Without it, his life upon the planet would be acutely and dangerously precarious.

Every time I go to walk upon the beach, I am reminded of this truth; before my eyes there lies irrefutable evidence of the great moisture cycle that pervades the earth. Every bit of driftwood, every wave-smoothed stone, every shining shell bears mute testimony that it has come from afar.

The basic building materials from which each of these was formed—whether wood or stone or shell—originated on the land, but was borne seaward by the waters that returned to the ocean from which they came. Every running river, every flowing stream, every bubbling spring that spills its fresh water into the sea, bears with it some plant material, some minerals, some silt, some basic shell-building ingredients that were leached, scoured, and lifted from the land.

The process is perpetual. It goes on relentlessly. Ocean to land, land to ocean. Water to soil and rock, soil and minerals back to the sea. At the mouth of every tiny stream, rivulet, giant glacier, or wide river, billions of tons of material are carried into the ocean every year. Huge estuaries of alluvial soil and silt steadily build up into the sea. At the outflow of rivers like the Nile and the Mississippi, they extend for miles and miles into the ocean. New land is formed in this fashion, to provide some of the most prized and fertile soil in all the world.

Yet for every ton of minerals made into new land, perhaps a hundred or two hundred tons is swept on out to sea. No one knows the exact proportion. There is no way to tell how many unmeasured millions of tons of material are gently deposited in the ocean deeps. There is no way man can even guess how the minerals of the earth have been deposited, layer upon layer, all across the great continental shelves that underlie the sea.

We know only that in the majestic, mysterious manner of great oceans in action, there

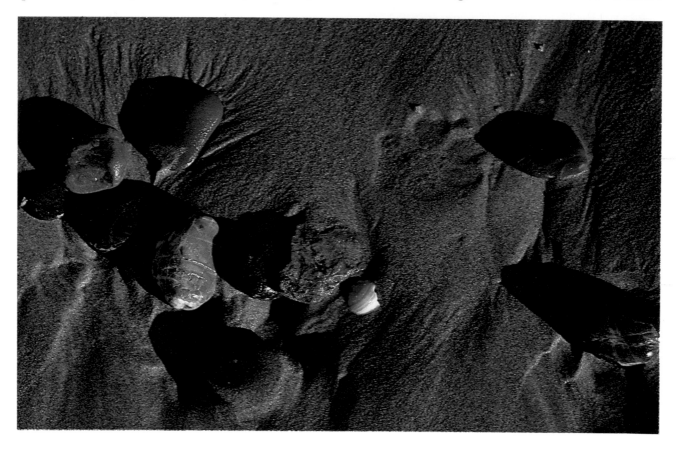

are dispersed—far and wide throughout its vast expanse—minerals in solution. It is in very truth a veritable storehouse of enormous wealth and bounty. Upon this largess an infinite multitude of flora and fauna fashion their unique life forms, to flourish in marvelous profusion.

Every empty seashell I pick up from the sand; every discarded worm case that tumbles in the tide; every fragile, feathery shard of broken coral on the reef; every shining particle of sand; every bit of bone or feather or skin of shark or seal lying along the sun-warmed shore, tells a story of moisture in motion, from sea to land, then back again.

In times of great storms and raging river floods, this whole process is dramatized. In a matter of days, we can see forces at work that ordinarily would take months or years to achieve the same results.

Trees and brush and roots are torn out of the riverbanks, to be swept out to sea. There they are tossed about and tumbled in the waves, later to be carried back to the coast and flung up on the shore. Eventually, at high tide, a long, tangled necklace of bleached and silvered driftwood lines the tide line.

In fierce floods, masses of mud and silt—scoured from streams and rivers—are picked up in the rushing torrents, to be carried far out into the ocean currents. It stains the sea for miles and miles. The land, like a wounded beast, seems to ooze blood, which flows away into the far reaches of the ocean depths. There the running currents and changing tides bear it away, until its life has been laid down in a last deposit amid the slime and mud of the ocean floor.

The same giant storms that brought teeming rain and flash floods to the land will also have stirred the ocean surface with gigantic gales. Enormous waves—some of them as much as fifty or sixty feet from trough to crest and roughly seven times as much in length—surge across the sea. No man has ever accurately measured the mightiest waves. It has been guessed that at times they may reach or even exceed one hundred feet. No one really knows. It depends upon the fetch of the wind and the force of the gale.

When those tremendous, towering breakers burst in full fury upon the flooded coasts, there is the supreme and indisputable demonstration of the ocean cycle in action. Windows and roofs of lighthouses more than 200 feet above the tide have been shattered and smashed by raging seas.

Some of the titanic waves toss rocks and boulders hundreds of feet into the air, smashing buildings, eroding cliffs. Rocks rumble in the surf. The waves thunder like a giant hammer mill, pulverizing all the debris dumped into their maw by the racing streams and rivers. At such moments, man stands back and watches from afar. His spirit is stilled, his soul is stirred.

In such settings of spectacular power, there come ringing the magnificent refrains from the pen of the psalmist:

> Bless the Lord, O my soul. O Lord my God, thou art very great; thou art clothed with honour and majesty. Who coverest thyself with light as with a garment: who stretchest out the heavens like a curtain: Who layeth the beams of his chambers in the waters: who maketh the clouds his chariot: who walketh upon the wings of the wind.
>
> Psalms 104:1–3

As year follows year, as century follows century, the ocean never ceases from its gigantic task of redistributing the mineral resources of the earth. On the average there are roughly some 160 million tons of dissolved salts in every cubic mile of seawater. The ocean holds this vast accumulation of solids in a liquid solution. Seawater is totally different from the fresh water of the streams and rivers flowing into it, whose minerals, leached and eroded from the land, are held in suspension.

The materials carried by the ocean water are picked up by marine flora and fauna in complex processes, which even our most-sophisticated scientists have not yet been able to fully understand or explain. We really do not know how ocean organisms can extract huge quantities of calcium from seawater, to fashion their own intricate and complex life forms. Seashells, corals, and body casings of a hundred sorts abound in the ocean deeps.

/109

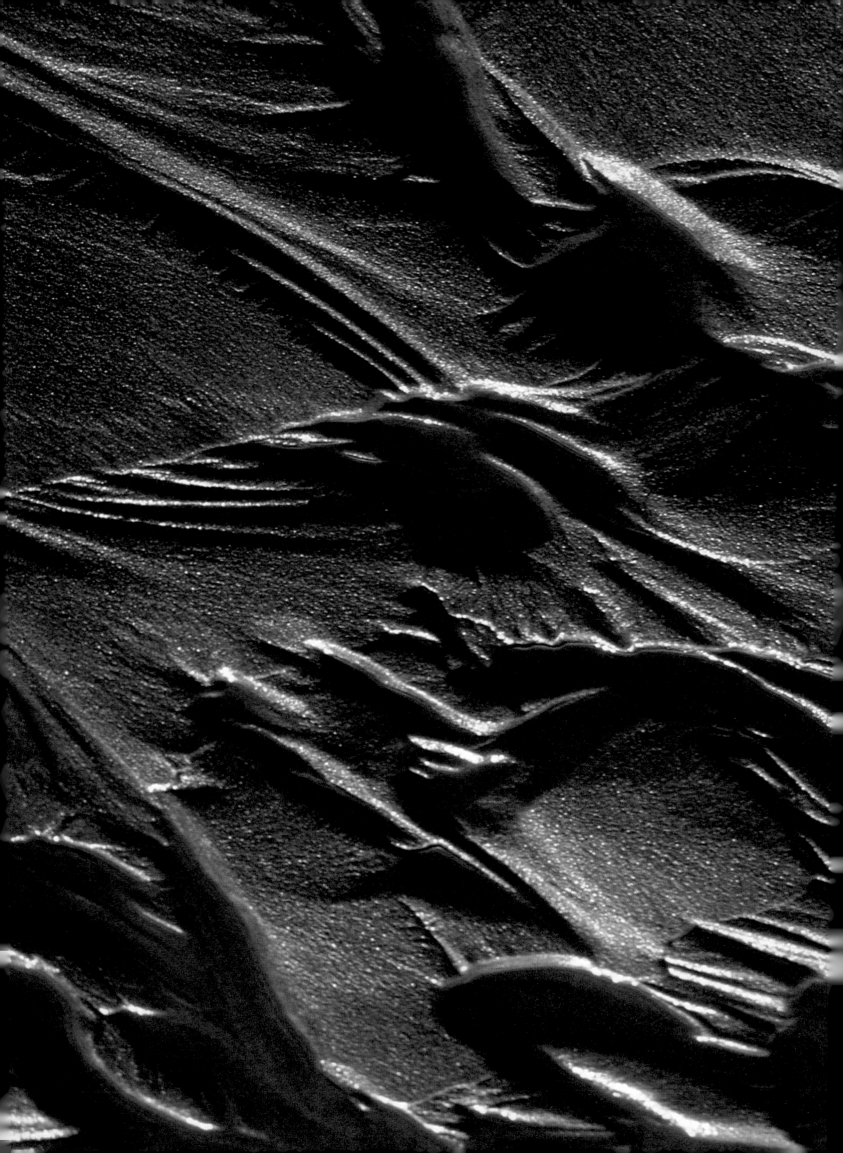

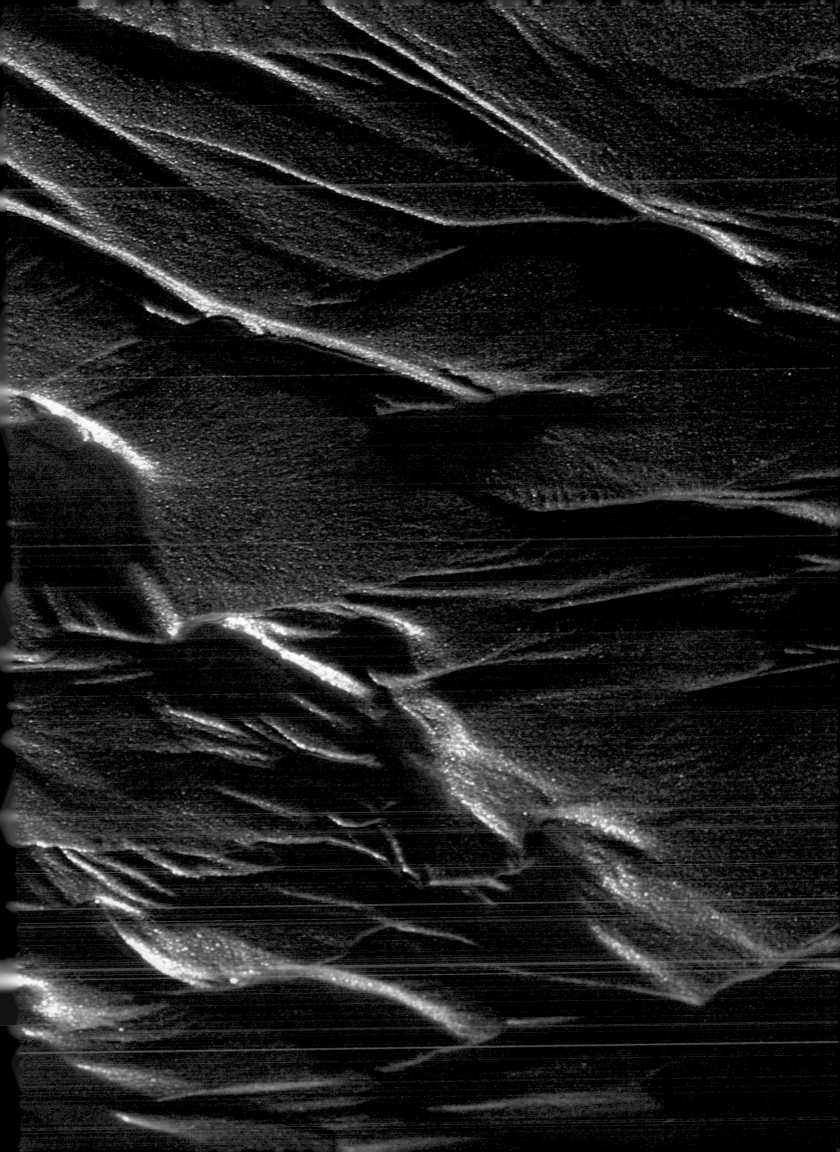

It is fortunate indeed that this does happen. It is one of the ways in which minerals are redistributed around the globe. The gradual growth of great reefs, the intricate and complex formation of fabulous submarine forests of kelp and weeds, the migration of masses of marine organisms from one part of the ocean to another, are all ongoing movements of minerals in the sea.

Yet steadily, surely, the ocean's mineral wealth is added to annually. The eruption of volcanoes on the seabed sends millions of tons of molten minerals into the ocean depths. Even the falling of rain, which is charged with particles of windblown dust from off the continents, deposits millions of tons of material in the sea.

Very little of this ever finds its way back to land. It is true that in a very heavy blow, with high seas running and the wind whipping spray and spume off the whitecaps, some sea salts will become airborne and carried inland. There are, for example, estimates that the British Isles receive an average of twenty-five pounds of sea salt per acre per year. But this is minimal, compared with the thousands of tons of material washed from her land to the sea every year.

The net result across the centuries has been for the ocean to become steadily more briny. In waters where air temperatures above the sea are very high and moisture evaporation is very rapid, the oceans become intensely salty. A classic and well-known case in point is the Red Sea, lying in its hot trench between Africa and Arabia. So saline is this sea that even a novice swimmer is impressed with its extraordinary bouyancy, to say nothing of its intense pungency. Wherever it dries, on the skin or any other surface, it leaves behind a white deposit of minerals.

Now this mineral content of the sea is much more than mere salt. It is an extremely complex mixture, containing almost every element known upon the planet. Depending upon the location of any given body of water, its content varies to an astonishing degree. And, strange as it may seem, the ocean is a veritable treasure house of minerals that man often finds very rare and difficult to obtain on land.

Three diverse and unusual elements will serve to illustrate this point. The first is gold. This rare and precious metal actually occurs in the ocean in vast yet unmeasured quantities. It has been estimated that there is more than enough gold in the sea to make every man, woman, and child a millionaire.

The difficulty is finding a feasible and economic process to extract it from the ocean. The quantity of gold found in salt water varies from place to place. German scientists, especially, have devoted an enormous amount of time, thought, and research to the extraction of gold from the ocean.

There is no question that, if the price of gold should continue to escalate as it has in recent years, the point will be reached where its extraction from the ocean storehouse will become economically feasible and practical. It will then become a major industry.

Magnesium is another remarkable material that occurs in the earth's oceans in prodigious supply. It is known that every cubic mile of seawater carries roughly 4 million tons of magnesium. This is a figure that astonishes me. It gives an inkling of just how vast is the treasure trove of the sea around us.

Magnesium, since the advent of aircraft, has become one of the most-strategic metals

known to modern man. Because of its light weight, its strength, and its durability under stress, it plays a major role in the manufacture of airplanes. All the larger military and commercial aircraft require anywhere up to half a ton of magnesium in their construction. By far, the greatest part of the supply for this purpose is derived from the sea.

This magnesium is also used in such diverse products as printer's ink, medications, ammunition, toothpaste, and incendiary bombs. It has been found to be one of the most essential and beneficial materials for the human eye. Bountiful supplies of magnesium in the diet assure excellent eye health. A ready source for this is dolomite, which can be found in almost any drugstore.

A third interesting element that occurs in the ocean is iodine. For reasons not yet clearly understood, most living forms incorporate iodine into their makeup. So much so is this the case that the general health of many organisms is directly related to iodine. They have become deeply dependent upon it for general health and well-being. In humans we find iodine to be essential for the proper function of the thyroid gland, which in turn controls the rate of body metabolism.

Sources of iodine on land are exceedingly rare and often very difficult to develop. Yet iodine occurs freely and abundantly in the earth's oceans. It is an important ingredient in many forms of marine growth, especially the seaweeds and kelps from which it has been derived for centuries. The pungent aroma of ozone off the sea is redolent with iodine. At low tide, with sun warming the exposed mud flats and shallow bays, the smell of iodine in the air is powerful, pronounced, and profoundly invigorating.

The rather remarkable and intriguing aspect to all of the enormous mineral wealth of the ocean is the apparent difficulty man has had in extracting any great amount for commercial purposes. This is doubly so when we pause to consider the incredible expertise of the invertebrate organisms that extract it for their own use. Human beings, especially those of the scientific community, tend to exult in their achievements and pride themselves upon their expertise in unlocking the secrets of the earth. But in large measure they have been baffled by the complex chemistry of the oceans.

Of course, in recent years, a much more concerted effort has been made to study and understand the seas. Only now is the fascinating field of oceanography truly coming into its own. Many scientists consider the ocean to be man's last great frontier upon the planet. The discoveries made there almost match those of outer space. By and large, man has only been familiar with the surface of the sea to a depth of a few fathoms. The ocean deeps remained a dark, foreign, forbidding region, explored by only a tiny handful of daring and audacious adventurers.

There is no question that as time goes on and modern oceanography opens new concepts or devises new techniques for understanding the ocean, it will prove to be a veritable storehouse of wealth. This is not only because of its capacity to hold mineral wealth, but also because of its ability to produce a profusion of life forms, some of which may well contribute to the survival of the proliferating human race upon the planet.

A typical demonstration of this has been the recent discovery of enormous oil and gas deposits beneath the ocean floor. Just how these have been formed is still a matter of theory, speculation, and conjecture. Nonetheless, the fact remains that the petroleum and gas reserves of the world have been the grand and glorious work of the ocean across millenia. Today that productivity heats our homes, fuels our factories, works our farms, transports us swiftly across oceans, land, and skies.

All of this is an integral and inescapable part of the ocean's glory. She has bequeathed us, under God's good hand, a bounty beyond our wildest expectations.

killed in enormous numbers has startled society. Perhaps it is not too late to hope that, by means of international treaties and limitations of kill, at least a small surviving remnant of each species can be preserved, to repopulate the oceans.

Intimate, detailed, even loving studies of whales are now being made by young men and women who have quite literally learned to adore and admire their giant, gentle friends. When they speak of their close encounters with these great denizens of the deep, it is always with enormous awe, reverence, and respect. Otherwise-hard-boiled scientists resort freely to such romantic language as, "These are the most graceful creatures on the planet." Or, "There is a strength, tenderness, tolerance, and goodwill apparent in these animals that man has so savagely mutilated across the years."

It has impressed me how concerned the scientific community has become to insure the preservation of not only whales, but all forms of sea life. It parallels the aroused conservation cause that endeavors to protect all endangered species on land. I am deeply touched in spirit to see men and women who will personally give their very lives to protect the whales off Maui, in Hawaii, from the speeding hydrofoil ferries. It is no less stirring than the self-sacrifice of game wardens and wildlife conservationists in Kenya, who are struggling to save the remaining elephant herds from poachers.

Obviously those concerned have discovered and are completely convinced that this particular life form deserves protection from the ruthless exploitation of man. Somehow a deep and profound sense of reverence for life is taking root in the conscience of late-twentieth-century society. There are some who will sneer at this. They ask, rather naively and callously, "What does it matter if they do become extinct? Who cares?"

Fortunately there are a dedicated minority who do care. And in this caring lies a glimmer of hope for all of us. For it is when men no longer care that darkness and despair and degradation descend quickly over society. Whether we wish to recognize it or not, all of us are impoverished, even if only to a small degree, by extinguishing of any life form on the planet.

If we pursue only the path of plunder in dealing with our fellow creatures, we must conclude that the time will come when no birds will sing in our skies, no wild animals will grace our forests and plains, no mammals or fish will roam our oceans. We will be left with a forlorn environment, stripped and shorn of its glory. Man may endeavor to replace it with the superficial substitutes of his own plastic manufacturing, but the best of his efforts remain lifeless and nonreproductive. They will stand in open mockery of the wild glory he has lost.

I have stood alone—silent, watching, listening—waiting for the sound of the whales as they passed offshore. I have done this on the chill northern coasts of Canada. I have done it on the cliffs of California and Anacapa Island. I have done it on the sun-warmed shores of Hawaii.

Every time the great animals blow or breach or fling their fantastic flukes into the sky, I am stirred by the sound of their going. Their migration may well take them four, five, or even six thousand miles across the ocean depths, from their southern calving grounds to the luxuriant summer-feeding areas of the arctic seas. It is a tremendous drama, of which we know very little. As they travel, they sing and call and whistle to one another in a surprising symphony of sound.

Some of this has been recorded for us. It has been taped and played over our radio stations and television programs. It is our rather childish, human way of saying, "What have you got to tell us? We're listening." At best we understand very little; we comprehend only dimly; our receptivity is blurred.

The Scriptures, written so long, long ago, bear enduring testimony to this. In touching, moving language, the book of Job, the oldest in the Bible and first ever written, declares:

> But none saith, Where is God my maker, who giveth songs in the night; Who teacheth us more than the beasts of the earth, and maketh us wiser than the fowls of heaven? There they cry, but none giveth answer, because of the pride of evil men.
>
> Job 35:10–12

Across the long centuries of human history, man has, in his ignorance, superstition, and fear, fabricated all sorts of weird and distorted concepts about ocean monsters. "Dragons of the deep," "great sea serpents," "mermaids" and other such creatures have been either imagined or reported. Poets and bards and minstrels have written and sung stories about them. Legends have been passed on from generation to generation. The myths persist even to this day, many of them grounded in ignorance.

Yet, on the other hand, from time to time rare and unusual specimens of unknown species are brought up from the deep. They excite the public imagination and stimulate renewed interest in the idea of unknown monsters.

Just a few weeks ago, while strolling beside the sea, I was startled by the appearance of a long, dark, sinuous object moving among the waves. At first glance it gave the distinct impression of a serpentine creature, with rather large, black, shiny coils, undulating through the breakers. Momentarily, it appeared to be a live creature that had surfaced near the shore.

But, as I drew near, I saw that it was in fact a very long, slender, shiny tree trunk that had been borne out to the ocean in a winter storm. Shorn and stripped of all its branches, bark, and leaves, it had turned dark and smooth and snakelike in the seawater. Its shape and size was such that each wave passing under it turned and rotated it in a most-convincing, sinuous, serpentine movement. So I, like hundreds of other observers across the centuries, had seen a "sea serpent."

Other sea creatures that have excited the interest of man are the lesser mammals: the seals, the sea lions, walrus, dolphins, and sea otters, to name but a few. Some of these spend a portion of their time on land—or on the ice, in polar regions. They come out of the ocean to expose themselves to view or they travel in company with ships.

Several places, which are among my favorite spots to walk along the Pacific shore, have "seal rocks" lying just beyond the low-tide mark. These outcrops are covered with barnacles and black, shiny, razor-sharp colonies of mussels. Every high tide sweeps over them in a cascading foam of rushing water. But as soon as the sea recedes, the rocks become exposed again. It is then that the seals and sea lions struggle, grunt, and shove themselves up onto their slippery surfaces to sun themselves.

It is a rather hilarious performance, because no sooner are they comfortably settled, than an unusually large wave will come rolling in to sweep them off their sun deck. In

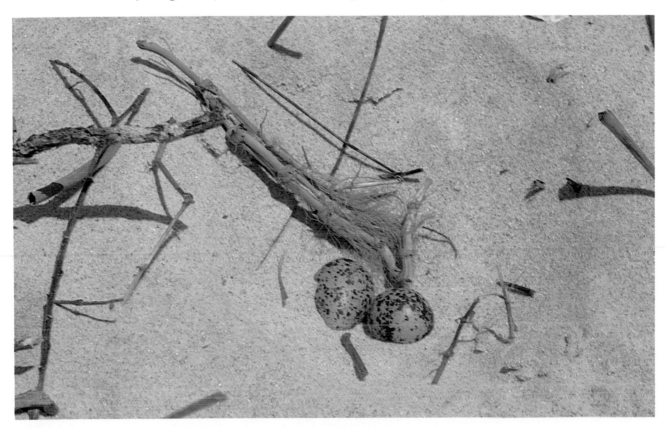

desperation, they lift their heads and twist their posteriors, to lessen the impact of the breaker. Sometimes they succeed. Other times they are rolled off the rocks, to be buried in the foam again.

They are persistent fellows, returning again and again and again, determined to enjoy their day in the sun. The rivalry and competition for the most-comfortable spot is amusing to watch. They push, shove, and slither about with tremendous exertion. The largest and most-powerful members generally manage to ensconce themselves on the highest points. All this heaving and struggling for "prior place" is a repetition of the pecking order that runs all through life. It is accompanied by grunting, moaning, and threatening demonstrations.

Sometimes the rocks are shared by seabirds. Gulls and cormorants especially favor such convenient perches. One day I was doubled up with laughter at the angry reaction of outraged protest shown by one old bull, who objected mightily when a bleary-eyed cormorant unwittingly lit on his back. It was as if an ocean monarch had been insulted. His indignation was immense. He writhed, twisted, and tossed his head angrily to shake off the frightened bird.

When both the black cormorants and the dark-bodied seals decide to use the seal rocks at the same time, the whole surface is literally alive with sea life. On occasion the seals crowd themselves so tightly together that there is scarcely room for a bird to set foot. More often than not, the cormorants will leave and fly to the cliffs onshore, where their rest is less disturbed by their thick-skinned neighbors.

For me, the seabirds are especially exciting. Somehow they share the shoreline with

me in an intimate and winsome way. It is as though this is very much *our* world—a world of land, sea, and air from which all of us derive enormous benefit. Ocean birds, on the whole, impress me with the vigor of their life; the clean, clear movement of their flight; the intensity of their search for sustenance from the sea; the sublime serenity of their adaptation to the ocean.

The seabirds have taught me many lessons in patience, perseverance, acceptance, and initiative. But more than this, they have enriched my ocean days beyond my ability to express in human language. As long as there are white-winged gulls sailing in the wind over the waves; as long as curlews call across the sands; as long as pelicans plunge between the breakers, snatching fish from the sea, all cannot be wrong with the world.

Anyone who studies seabirds in detail can never help but be impressed by the hardiness of their habits and the vastness of the range over which some of them roam the ocean. There are species, such as some of the curlews, which spend the summer nesting on the arctic tundra of Alaska's north slope and Canada's arctic islands. Yet their fall migrations take them thousands of miles down the eastern seaboard, across the Caribbean, along South America's coast, to the southern shores of Argentina and Peru.

These are incredible journeys, calling for enormous endurance. Yet the unpretentious brown birds, with their curving sickle beaks, stroll nonchalantly up and down the sand flats of the beach before my windows without pretense or fanfare. Every time I watch them, each standing on one leg, head tucked beneath wing, mirrored in the shining wetness of the sand, I am quietly impressed with their composure. Just their presence on the beach is proof of the remarkable migrations imperative for perpetuation of the species, for now they are headed north, along the Pacific.

Of course this cannot be said for all seabirds. The world over, hunters and egg collectors and plumage peddlers have taken a terrible toll of seabirds. In some cases, whole species have been endangered. Yet, by degrees, awareness and enlightenment have

begun to penetrate the conscience of an aroused society. In many countries there are now rigid regulations and strict controls over the killing or capture of seabirds.

Sometimes, as I walk along the edge of the tide line, the curlews and willet and whimbrels dart about ahead of me. They run in and out, over the white wash of waves, probing in the wet sand for marine life. This they do with speed and dexterity, driving their saberlike bills into the sand like powerful little pneumatic drills.

Then suddenly a flight of them will lift off into the wind. They move in unison, their gorgeous golden-bronze plumage shining in the setting sun. Their thin, haunting, plaintive cries carry across the breeze-blown beach. It is the call of wide seas, of wild ocean winds, of the northern tundra. It is the salute to a sturdy species.

The seabirds have always called me to the coastlines of the world. I am less attracted by the minute technical details of their majestic movements across the globe than I am by the sheer beauty of their flight, the freedom of their life-style, the haunting inspiration of their cries, the uplift of spirit and stirring of my soul that their presence invokes. This is not to be merely poetic or romantic, for the birds of the sea speak to me, in unmistakable language, of the loving care and powerful concern of my Father in heaven.

This world, this fragment of material spinning in space, is the object of His thought, His tender artistry, His careful preservation. Not only does He care about me as a man, but He cares, too, about the curlews, the pelicans, the plovers, the gulls, the grebes, the cormorants, and a score of other species that are silhouetted against the sunrises and sunsets of my skies. When He was here among us in human guise, He made it abundantly clear that not even a fledgling fell to the ground without His special, personal knowledge and concern for its welfare. This is His world. It is beautiful and inspiring and stimulating not by blind chance, but by His loving care and gracious generosity.

Even the presence of a golden plover, running daintily in the grass at the edge of a Hawaiian beach, is a glad reminder of the wonders of my Father's world. Here I quote in part from my book *Hawaiian Interlude*. I do so without apology, for it endorses today exactly what I felt and knew and sensed in those far-off days when Hawaii was my home:

The golden plover was an equally astonishing bird. Those I saw along the grassy patches of shoreline were migrants in the islands. Already, though, they had taken up territory on shore after their long flight across the far reaches of the Northern Pacific from their nesting grounds on the Alaska tundra. The return flight of fledgling golden plovers, a land bird, across nearly 2,000 miles of open ocean to find footing again on these pinpoints of land in mid-Pacific is perhaps the most magnificent migration feat of any bird upon the planet.

During the return migration in autumn, the male plovers are the first to fill the evening and morning skies with their haunting, high-pitched cries. Especially on moonlit nights, one can hear them calling to their flying companions as they wing in over the islands from the far north.

The female birds and fledglings follow a little later. The young birds and their attendant mothers require a little longer on the tundra to accumulate enough body fat to fuel their long flight southwards. In flight about two ounces of this fat is oxidized by the bird's body for both energy and water to maintain body metabolism on the wing.

Tests have been made by ornithologists to determine if plovers, a distinct land bird, can possibly rest on the sea. Though the bird can float on the water it cannot take off from the surface, proving beyond doubt that the entire trans-Pacific flight of approximately 2,000 miles is made non-stop. These birds can fly at sixty miles an hour or better, but assuming that they cruised

leisurely at forty miles an hour, the over-water journey would mean some fifty hours of continuous, non-stop rapid wing action. A fantastic feat of endurance for bone, blood and muscle to perform.

As I followed the rather inconspicuous little plover across the grassy sward between the lava rocks I meditated much on their life habits. That a small bird of their proportions could, without previous experience or knowledge, migrate through storms, wind, sleet, snow and rain for two thousand miles unerringly over open ocean was a majestic mystery. (I care not how much scientists may endeavour to explain away such an astonishing achievement.) The more so when it is remembered that such amazing capacities for calculating wind-drift, latitude, speed of flight and physical endurance must all be bound up in the tiny particle of a single sperm cell and a single egg cell which ultimately becomes a fulfledged wonder of flight.

There are many who simply assume, rather naively, I think, that such phenomena are the product of mere chance. It requires a great deal of blind faith to believe this. Certainly much more than it does to have the simple, honest, intellectual humility to acknowledge the "master mind" of a benevolent Creator at work behind the scenes in an ordered universe.

Less conspicuous, less obvious, less easily seen are the innumerable species of fish to be found in the oceans of the world. Those who pursue them, either for food, sport, or commerce, of course are ever aware of their presence in the sea. There are literally thousands of species. Some of them, such as the giant swordfish, can put on spectacular displays when hooked. The mass migrations of uncounted millions of salmon up coastal rivers and streams can stir our excitement. The shining silver hordes of tuna, herring, and anchovies sustain formidable fishing fleets.

The ocean abounds with marine life of a myriad sort. Anyone who spends even a casual hour or two exploring a tide pool cannot help but marvel at the diversity of sea forms found in such a small compass. If perchance the pool is in the warm waters of some tropical lagoon, there will be brilliant, multicolored fish of all kinds. Sea urchins, sea anemones, and sea snails of diverse sorts will make this their habitat. The array of algae, mosses, corals, starfish, and shells will stagger a stranger.

There is no possible way in which even a small fraction of all ocean life can be described in a book of this kind. The waters of the world's oceans proliferate with myriads of marine forms, which vary in color, shape, size, and habit—from the sup-

posedly ordinary barnacle on a boat to the most-complex, electrically charged, self-illuminating creatures of the ocean deeps.

The various animal life of the ocean has taken on thousands of unique characteristics, which admirably suit it to some highly specialized life-style in some certain segment of the sea. There are creatures with scales, some with skin, some with shells, some with horny skeletons, some with spines, some with only slimy forms. The variety is endless. The diversity is multitudinous. The range of colors is beyond belief.

Those enthusiasts who enjoy skin diving, submarine studies, and underwater exploration rave about the eye-boggling beauty of the ocean depths. In places there are deep canyons, complex caverns, enormous reefs, and lovely lagoons, where sea life beyond any artist's wildest fancy flourishs in colorful profusion. It is a realm of rare beauty and wondrous tranquility.

Here sea life of a thousand kinds have adjusted to one another in beautiful balance. Sea ferns, corals, fish, crustaceans, and graceful fronds of seaweeds; all are part of a shifting, changing, pulsing panorama that is sustained by the food-bearing, drifting ocean currents. In beautiful paintings, brilliant photographs, breathtaking films, a small part of this ocean glory has been reproduced.

Magazines, books, films, and photographs of a hundred sorts have shown the unending splendor of the ocean's glory. The undersea gardens of the world rival the beauty of mountain alp lands and desert flowers after winter rains. They are a spectacle of wonder and awe, which comparatively few people have the privilege to observe in real life. But those who do, become completely enamored with the marine fairylands that occur in

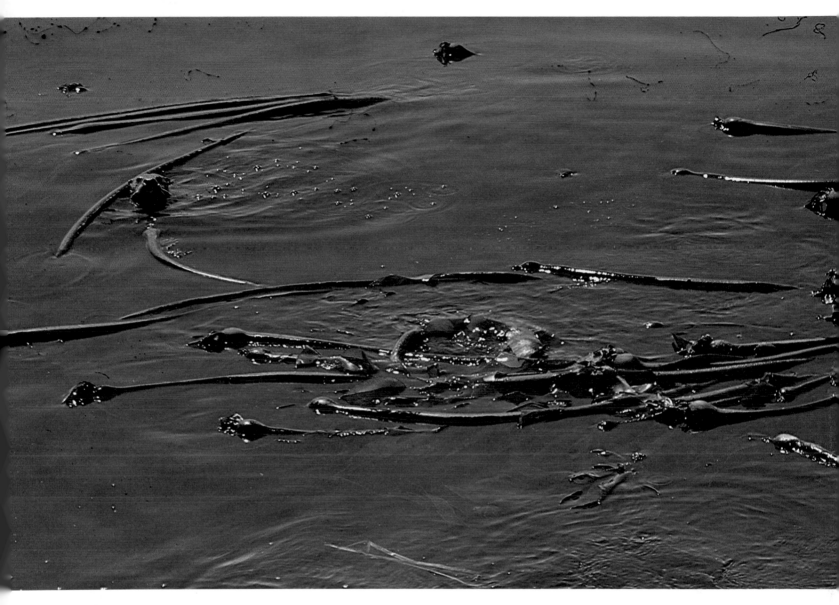

some parts of the undersea world.

Basic to all of this lies the fundamental food supply of the ocean—plankton. It has been well said that plankton is to the sea what grass and plants are to the land. It is the all-pervasive common denominator upon which all other marine life ultimately depends for survival. It is the ubiquitous, basic, life-building material that underlies the entire complex pyramid of biological functions in the ocean. It is that which maintains and sustains the whole web of life in the sea.

There are in actual fact uncounted myriads of forms of plankton found in the ocean. They are so small in size, so minute in scale, that massed millions of them are microscopic in size. They cannot be seen with an unaided human eye. Yet at other times their sheer numbers are so enormous, and they proliferate so profusely, that they can color the ocean currents. The sudden appearance of the ominous, poisonous red tide is an example of this.

Roughly speaking, plankton are divided into two general classes. The most common are the so-called diatoms. These are actually minute marine plants that thrive in the colder waters of the world's seas. Depending upon temperatures, water currents, sunlight, and availability of plant nutrients welling up from the ocean floor, they either proliferate or diminish in number. These microscopic plants comprise about 90 percent of all plankton.

The remaining 10 percent are the so-called plankton "animals." These are numerous in form, but most commonly represented by dinoflagellates. Included in this class of plankton are the tiny copepods, which are related to lobsters and crabs.

The plankton are screened out of the sea by fish and sea animals as a primary source of food. Small fish that do this are in turn pursued and eaten by larger fish, mammals, birds, or men. So it may be seen that eventually all ocean life is either directly or indirectly dependent upon plankton.

It has been suggested that this basic protein supply offers mankind the greatest alternative food resource remaining upon the planet. Marine biologists debate this idea, because it has yet to be demonstrated that we can devise a system as efficient as that of fish and sea mammals for harvesting plankton from the ocean. Just as the most-primitive crustaceans are more efficient than man's finest chemists in removing minerals from the sea, likewise lower forms of marine life are better able to utilize plankton as a source of protein than any sophisticated system so far designed by our scientific ingenuity.

This is an important concept for us to grasp. For though the ocean spreads out before us as a gigantic banquet table, still virtually untouched, teeming with billions upon billions of tons of plankton, no truly efficient means for partaking of this bounty has been found. Perhaps eventually the proliferating human population will compel men to devise some way of harvesting this so-called "sea grass" directly from the ocean currents.

Whatever the future may hold, for the present, we look out upon the ocean in quiet wonder. It is more—much more—than a mighty mass of water lying inert within its giant planetary basins. It is in truth a living, pulsing, moving, dynamic embodiment of myriad life forms. Within the oceanic environment, they live and move and have their being. Permeating every particle of this entire ecosystem are design, order, beauty, interdependence, and majestic mystery still beyond the mind of man to fully understand.

As with the writer of ancient times, we still declare in sincerity, humility, and intellectual integrity:

> And God created great whales, and every living creature that moveth, which the waters brought forth abundantly, after their kind, and every winged fowl after his kind: and God saw that it was good. And God blessed them, saying, Be fruitful, and multiply, and fill the waters in the seas, and let fowl multiply in the earth.
>
> Genesis 1:21, 22

And God said,
Let us make man in our image,
after our likeness: and let them have
dominion over the fish of the sea,
and over the fowl of the air,
and over the cattle,
and over all the earth,
and over every creeping thing
that creepeth upon the earth.
So God created man in his own image,
in the image of God created he him;
male and female created he them.
And God blessed them,
and God said unto them,
Be fruitful, and multiply,
and replenish the earth, and subdue it:
and have dominion
over the fish of the sea,
and over the fowl of the air,
and over every living thing
that moveth upon the earth.

Genesis 1:26 - 28

7

Man and the Ocean

In the Introduction to this book, it was emphasized that in large measure it was the account of my own passionate love affair with the sea. In the preceding pages has been recorded the remarkable impact the ocean has made upon the life of one man. It is my sincere hope and earnest prayer that some of the inspiration, some of the pleasure, some of the awe, some of the unforgettable delights that the seas have bestowed upon me will have been passed on, to enrich the reader. It is my desire that some may have come to a fresh awareness that the ocean is indeed a wondrous part of our Father's world.

If in fact this has happened, then this final segment of the book will be of much greater significance. For the fact remains that, increasingly, man is having an enormous impact upon the ocean. For long centuries the seas seemed so vast, so extensive, so overwhelming that it was simply assumed they would remain the same indefinitely. Puny men, in their relative ignorance and shortsightedness, abused and misused the ocean and its resources with utter impunity. Some of this may have been done in gross ignorance; some certainly was carried out with crass carelessness; some was done with deliberate greed for gain; and some was straightforward stupidity.

It has not been anything but a patchwork story, in which there are intermingled lights and shadows, losses and gains, great honors and dark disasters.

Literally thousands of books have been written about man's exploration of the sea, about his commerce on the ocean; about his wars and battles above and beneath the waves; about his fishing, whaling, and sealing expeditions; about his use of the natural resources of the sea; about his boats and ships and oceangoing vessels of a hundred sorts; about his pleasures and pastimes on the ocean edge.

Through much of this recorded history, there runs a thread of romance. An element of adventure and deering-do dances upon many pages. There is the distinct impression that the ocean is man's final frontier upon the planet. Its depths, its mystery, its incredible resources, lure and draw him with enormous fascination. The seas are even regarded by some as our only guarantee of survival as a race.

With the accelerating advance of twentieth-century technology, it is becoming increasingly obvious that in terms of time and space, the seas really are not as immense as was once supposed. The ocean is not an overwhelming, inexhaustible, indestructible segment of our environment. To our terror, we are beginning to realize that we can wreak irreparable ruin on the ocean. We are discovering that the seas can be so polluted and contaminated with our industrial and commercial wastes that they will no longer sustain their own unique ecosystems. We are finding, to our dismay, that the supposedly endless natural resources of ocean life can be depleted to the point of no return and final dark extinction.

Fortunately for both the sea and ourselves, this general awareness is dawning upon us before totally irreparable damage has been done. Conservation of ocean resources today is every bit as acute in the social consciousness of maritime nations as is land conservation. We are waking up to the fact that man's impact upon his marine environment is critical to his own survival. And it must be added here that by that I mean much more than mere physical survival. For it is from the sea that there comes enormous moral and emotional well-being, as well as spiritual inspiration.

It is not surprising to see the tremendous interest shown in enacting legislation that will to some extent protect the ocean and its marine life from excessive predation by the human species. Approximately 100 countries have ocean frontage, from which their residents go out to exploit the sea. A massive number of treaties, compacts, and laws have been enacted to try and control man's activities in the ocean.

Of these, the most grandiose by far is the much-debated, hotly contested, and still-

unresolved "Law of the Sea." For more than five full years, scientists, politicians, statesmen, and legislators from around the globe have struggled with this titanic task in the Third United Nations' Conference on the Law of the Sea.

It is commonly recognized that their decisions influence approximately 70 percent of the earth's surface. The United Nations General Assembly has declared the ocean to be "The common heritage of mankind." Thus it belongs to all nations, not just those which may boast a seaboard.

It will be apparent why the debates drag on as they do. Who is to decide who shall have the privilege of extracting gigantic wealth from the ocean floor? Who will determine how these resources shall be distributed? Who shall supervise the complex and costly industries that are bound to be developed by men in their relentless search for new resources?

There are some pessimists who feel the world community will never be able to reach a consensus on this extraordinarily complex subject. If not, then we may well expect to see, at the close of this century, unbridled oceanic exploitation, which would completely eclipse anything man ever did on land by way of devastating damage.

In the meantime, it is somewhat of a consolation to know that, through various international treaties and agreements, some restraint is being shown in the use of ocean resources. Limitations of all sorts, both national and international, have been imposed

upon the taking of fish, crustaceans, seals, whales, mollusks, and other forms of sea life. Enormous sums of money are now being spent on study and research into the life habits of marine organisms. In the light of data collected, intelligent and increasingly farsighted laws are being enacted to protect oceanic stocks.

It is just as important for the local seaside resident of a California village to be restricted in how many clams he will dig with a shovel and pail, as it is for a Japanese whaler to be controlled in his catch in the Antarctic. There is no reason why a salmon fisherman near shore should be allowed to behave like a hog in taking more than his quota of shining beauties than the deep-sea trawler is allowed to catch in the far reaches of the Pacific.

All of us are in this together. And it matters not whether it be the poor peasant with his little rowboat or the great factory fleet of a multimillion-dollar corporation; all of us need to recognize and respect the rights of others. Beyond this, we must have and hold some reverence for the life of the sea itself. It is not ours to waste or abuse.

The world over, there is an increasing awareness, especially among maritime nations, that the marine life of the sea, if not properly managed and respected, can be seriously depleted. It is rapidly dawning upon us that it is perfectly possible, with modern fishing methods using sophisticated technology, to literally ravage the ocean of its famous fish stocks. Some of the world's best-known fishing grounds now furnish only a fraction of the supply that formerly represented their enormous productivity.

Fishing fleets that in olden days were more or less restricted to home waters now cross the ocean with impunity, to harvest fish stocks along foreign shores. This has led to tremendous rivalry, bitterness, and in some cases outright war among competing fishing

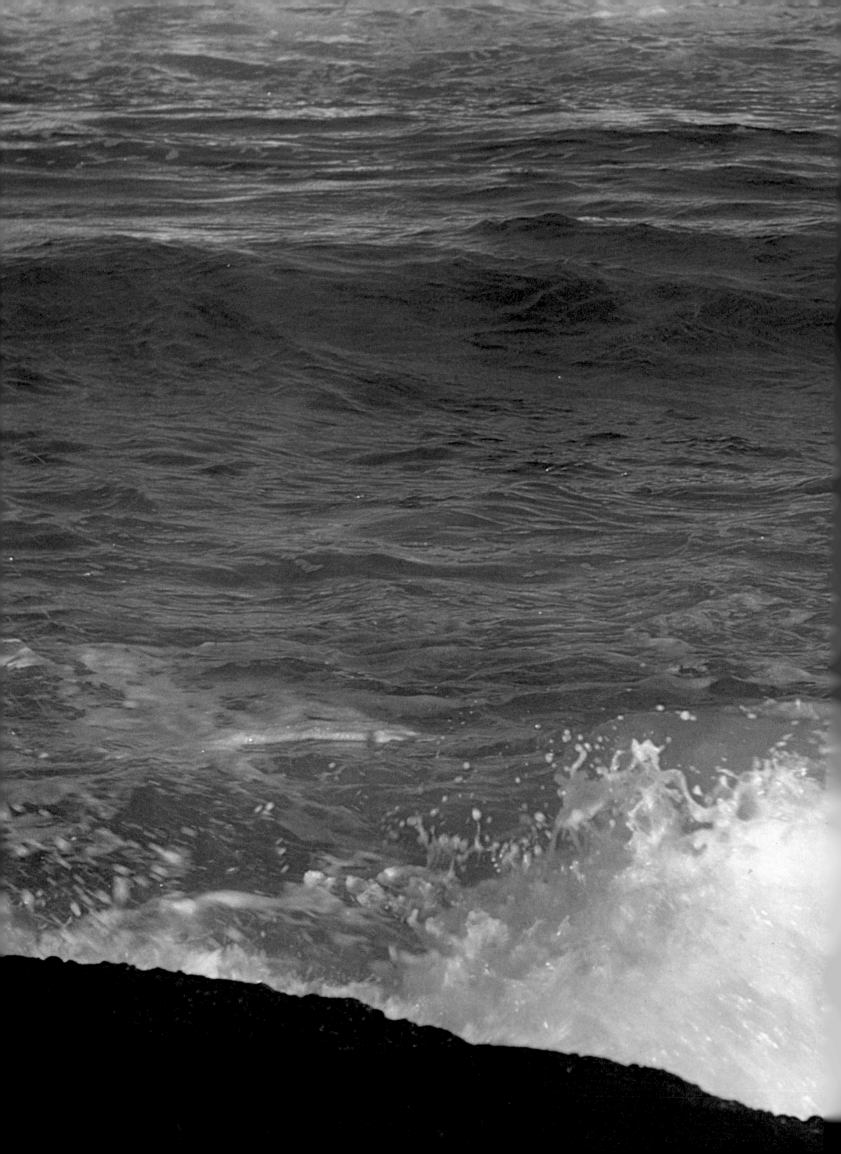

fleets. We receive reports of trawlers cutting one another's lines, ramming one another in midocean, and even firing on opponents.

The root cause, of course, is a diminishing supply of fish to feed an increasingly voracious market. By this I do not just refer to human consumption. The ever-increasing demands for fish meal, fish oil, and marine protein are quite literally insatiable, both for agricultural use of feeds and fertilizers as well as for commercial products as diverse as paint and perfume.

The annual harvest of fish from salt water exceeds 60 million tons. This is more than six times the catch taken from all fresh-water lakes, streams, and rivers. There are some marine biologists who believe that, with proper management, the ocean catch could be easily doubled or tripled. Others are less optimistic and feel that oceanic stocks are bound to decline, rather than increase.

The reason for the latter view is that, unlike with land, man's ability to use and manipulate the sea is at best minimal. Despite all the advances in our scientific methods, there is virtually nothing man can do to control ocean currents, to raise or lower the temperature of the sea, to increase or diminish its upwelling from the depths, to manipulate the winds blowing over its surface, or to control the clouds covering its great open expanses.

We may boast about our ability to influence weather. We may claim that we can control climate to a degree. We may dream of using atomic energy to generate the upwelling of nutritionally rich waters from the ocean floor. We may envisage grandiose schemes for altering and diverting ocean currents. But the sum total of our devices and designs ultimately is bound to be puny.

This is why some of the statements made in the Scriptures so long ago remain valid to this hour. If only we can, for a few sober moments, set aside our human arrogance and haughty scientific pride, we will concur with the writer of old, who penned these lines under the inspiration of God's own Spirit:

> Who hath measured the waters in the hollow of his hand, and meted out heaven with the span, and comprehended the dust of the earth in a measure, and weighed the mountains in scales, and the hills in a balance? Who hath directed the Spirit of the Lord, or being his counsellor hath taught him? With whom took he counsel, and who instructed him, and taught him in the path of judgment, and taught him knowledge, and shewed to him the way of understanding? Behold, the nations are as a drop of a bucket, and are counted as the small dust of the balance: behold, he taketh up the isles as a very little thing.
>
> Isaiah 40:12–15

None of the foregoing negates the solemn and sobering fact that man increasingly is bound to make an impact on the ocean. As with so many of our influences, the end result can be for good or evil. And it must be said here that, as enlightened people with a Christian conscience, we do have an obligation to care deeply about conservation of the oceanic environment.

It was pointed out emphatically in my book *Rabboni* that when there was delegated to man the enormous responsibility of having dominion over the resources of the sea (see

146/

Genesis 1:26–28), it was not a divine mandate to exploit it with impunity. Rather the very clear concept inherent in the mind of God was that, as He was a creator and conservator, so likewise should we, His children, created in His likeness, also be.

The very essence of the divine nature of God is love. Not a soft, sentimental sort of romantic euphoria. His love is the strong, sublime, supreme attribute of *caring,* to the point of utter selflessness and total self-giving, on behalf of that which is worth perpetuating. This is conservation at bedrock level. This is the profound caring of true love at its fundamental best. And, as Christians in the world community, we have a distinct obligation to care deeply about what happens to the ocean.

Without shame or embarrassment, we should not hesitate to express our concern over the depletion of ocean resources. We should be in the forefront of those who fight vigorously for the prevention of pollution and contamination of the seas. It is a trust bestowed upon us by our Father. This is His world, as well as ours.

For years without number, some men considered the ocean to be nothing more than a handy dumping ground for all their wastes and garbage. I shall never forget the rage that burned within my soul when I watched barge after barge of city refuse towed out to sea for dumping.

Clouds of seabirds would follow the piles of refuse, waiting for it to be spilled into the crystal-clear waters. As it sank slowly to the ocean floor, its filth and debris would stain the sea. More often than not, the next change of tide would carry a goodly portion of the garbage back onto the beach, where old tin cans, bottles, cartons, cloth, and discarded grapefruit skins littered the shoreline.

As if the insult of these solids were not enough, other communities simply ran their sewer pipes into the sea. Again the seabirds congregated around these outfalls, to gorge themselves on the despicable discharge of man's supposedly sophisticated society. To anyone with an iota of awareness or concern for the environment, it was an appalling performance. Believe it or not, it still goes on.

From time to time, some of the world's busiest beaches, lying close to great metropolitan centers, are closed to the public because of excess pollution. For fear of disease and epidemics of one kind or another, health officers will decide that the ocean no longer brings benefit, but rather an ominous hazard to its visitors.

The same principle applies to industrial discharges of all kinds that for years have been dumped into the ocean with utter disregard for the consequences. On the islands of Hawaii, it appalled me to see the ocean stained for miles and miles along the coast by the waste from the sugar mills. Thousands upon thousands of tons of silt, cane waste, and debris colored the blue Pacific a chocolate brown.

This debris, caught up in the waves, was washed back on miles of beach, suffocating the native marine life. The trash, lashing the rocks and beating the shoreline with a fierce scrubbing action, had literally stripped the coast of living organisms. Man had made a desert of desolation in the sea.

Out on the open ocean, ships of all sorts still, when they can do it without detection, dump their wastes in the water. Tankers used to consider it normal to clean their oil bunkers in any handy bay.

/147

So the list could go on and on of various ways in which a callous and indifferent society has abused the bounty of the world's oceans. Somehow, in our naive stupidity, we simply assumed that the sea would absorb and assimilate any insult we decided to discharge upon it!

To our sorrow and rather belated surprise, we have discovered that this simply is not so. Perhaps no other series of events so suddenly shocked and startled us wide awake to the damage we have done as did the breakup of great tankers at sea. When huge ships like the *Torry Canyon* or *Amaco Cadiz* spill thousands of tons of crude oil into the ocean in a single disaster, the whole world is suddenly alerted to the terrible path upon which we have set ourselves.

All over the world, beautiful beaches, gorgeous coastlines, and lovely seaside communities have been ravaged and ruined by oil washed up from the sea. The toll taken of seabirds and sea life is astronomical. The long-range results have yet to be tabulated or fully understood. Just because a cosmetic cleanup of the coast palliates the local populace does not mean that the enormous damage to marine life has been rectified.

It is not commonly known that oil has a peculiar capacity, when mixed with salt water, to slowly settle to the ocean floor. There it actually penetrates the silt and slime, creating an almost-indestructible fine film around every grain of sand or stone in the subsurface layers. There it is readily picked up and ingested by the lower marine organisms. They, in turn, when consumed, pass it on to ever-higher forms of predators that feed upon them in the food chain of the sea. The ultimate consequences, extending across months and years yet to come, may well be more terrifying and tragic than anything we have yet imagined, especially as the incidence of oil spills at sea and along our coasts increase.

Unless one has actually been at the scene of an oil spill, its impact on the senses is almost impossible to understand.

I was in Santa Barbara, California, during the winter of 1968–69, when oil, erupting from the oil drilling in the channel, washed up onto its beautiful beaches. I wrote about the epic events of that time at great length in my book *Travels of the Tortoise.*

The impact on the people of the city was heartrending. Men and women, boys and girls of all ages, walked up and down their beaches, blind with anger, heartbroken with grief. They picked up oil-soaked birds in boxes, bearing them away in hope of cleansing their plumage with detergent. They openly wept, especially some of the very young and very aged, who had learned to really love the seashore, now black with oil and sludge.

It took an enormous outlay of money, work, and planning to put things right again. And even yet, ten years later, there remains evidence that the damage done was much greater and more enduring then was imagined at the time.

The interrelated web of life in the ocean is much more complex, much more fragile, much more easily stressed and strained than we formerly believed. All of the living organisms within the ecosystem are too closely and irrevocably interdependent for one to be damaged without producing an enormous impact upon the others.

The ocean was not intended to be a convenient dump for the debris of man's wasteful society. To even consider it as such shows our appalling arrogance and abysmal stupidity. Yet it is surprising how hard it is to reverse our general attitudes on such matters.

148/

Perhaps the most preposterous example of this is the increasing use of the ocean for the disposal of both atomic wastes and the lethal debris from toxic chemicals. Strange and incongruous as it may sound, leakproof containers for such dreadful materials have yet to be designed. With utter impunity, men dump death-dealing wastes at sea, knowing full well that in the future they can escape, to pollute and endanger the whole environment.

It is not surprising that an aroused, angry, and militant number of conservationists are making themselves heard. How long must such utter madness be allowed?

As with waste disposal, so with ocean commerce and naval warfare. We appear to be a race victimized by expediency and compromise. It seems that as long as man's own selfish ends are served, he cares not what may become of the very earth upon which his own survival depends.

I am utterly appalled by the worldwide proliferation of nuclear-powered ships, submarines, and missiles. I have yet to see or read a single article, paper, or book where the issue is raised as to what will happen to the oceans of the world in the event of another global war.

In the event of such a holocaust, the sinking and shattering of literally hundreds of craft carrying atomic reactors and atomic warheads is certain. The escape of nuclear material into the sea and atmosphere will reach astronomical levels. Torpedoed ships, broken submarines, downed bombers, and shattered missiles—all bearing radioactive material in huge quantities—will contaminate the whole ocean with their leakage. Levels of radiation will be such as to exterminate most life in the sea.

What had been the earth's great glory could become her graveyard.

That military strategists, politicians, or naval architects even give such matters much thought is open to question. If they did, in their more-solemn moments of reflection, I doubt if they would pursue their present course. But most of us are shortsighted. We live, at best, for the moment, and the ravaged, embattled, beleaguered planet upon which we execute our selfishness bears mute testimony to the folly of our ways. How much longer it can sustain the insanity of our race is open to debate. We are set upon a course of diabolical self-destruction. The innocent stand by in silent apprehension and terror, not knowing when their demise will come.

It is not the sort of prospect to cheer men's spirits. And certainly it is even less for brazen men to brag about. The very military hardware in which nations put their confidence for containment of their so-called "enemies" may well prove to be the very means of their own ultimate demolition as a society.

These are sober reflections. As Christians, we have a serious obligation to consider them. We need to be bold enough to see where we are going and brave enough to voice our concern.

Fortunately for all of us, all that man does with the sea is not deleterious. There are some human activities that hold out great promise for the future, provided there is a future.

One of these is so-called sea farming. It is a science that has been given much greater attention in the Orient than in the Western world. Japan is devoting an enormous amount of energy, money, and research to the whole field of oceanic crops.

It has always impressed me how carefully the Japanese gather seaweed from the shore. When I lived in the South Pacific, they taught me to recognize the edible forms of marine growth that could be collected from the rocks at low tide. Some of these made nourishing soups and delicious side dishes, either as salads or sea vegetables. Sea lettuce became a special favorite, used to augment my diet.

Some marine biologists feel sure that the world's total production of food must eventually be increased through the culture of ocean organisms, both plant and animal. There will be exciting advances made in the management of coastal waters, salt marshes, mud flats, shallow bays, protected coves, and artificial lagoons, where sea farming can be carried on under carefully controlled conditions.

That this can be done has been amply demonstrated in the culture of pearls, the establishment of sophisticated oyster farms, the raising of food fish in man-made lagoons, and the cultivation of new species of crustaceans or mollusks in coastal waters

The ingenuity of man in this direction may prove to be one of the most exciting chapters in his history. It may well be as great an adventure and break with the past as when primitive man turned from being a hunter and forager to farming and the keeping of livestock. For up until only quite recently, human beings have used the ocean only as a hunting ground or field in which to forage for food. Now, at long last, the ocean is seen as an environment in which certain fixed colonies of marine life and crops of marine growth can be husbanded with skill and care.

Along with this, there is bound to be the twin development of using solar or tidal energy to convert seawater into fresh water. This is a realm offering enormous possibilities, for in the process, not only will a new supply of fresh water be provided for human consumption and irrigation of desert land, but also there will be the bonus of extracting vast quantities of minerals from the seawater during this process.

Some of these minerals can be applied directly to the soil as fertilizer, on the farms to be irrigated with the water from which they were extracted. Others can be used for a whole host of industrial purposes.

One of the ocean's great glories is her virtually untapped mineral wealth. All across the eons that her waters have encircled the globe, the sea has acted as the giant planetary bank, in which have been made innumerable deposits. Some came from the thousands of rivers, streams, and springs that carried minerals from the continents into the ocean. Others have come from the energy-conversion cycle, wherein the decomposing forms of marine life were deposited in the sea. Others were brought by rain and wind, in the form of fine dust and microscopic particles of soil and vegetation scoured off the land by weathering.

Only now are serious studies and daring industries being developed to make large withdrawals of these deposits from the sea. In former times the majority of people who lived by the ocean were content to extract a little salt, some dolomite, a bit of limestone or clamshell, and perhaps a few pounds of trace minerals not easily found on land, such as iodine.

All of this will change dramatically. Huge extractive industries are in the offing. Enormous sums of money are now being spent to design undersea equipment that will rival anything the oil industry has done to explore for oil and gas. New types of submarine equipment are being tested for oceanic exploration and deep-sea mining.

In the years to come, gems as scarce as diamonds, minerals as rare as gold and silver, huge quantities of copper, magnesium, and cobalt, to name but a few, will be taken from the ocean. It will be a whole new world, charged with enormous excitement and rewarded with huge returns in unimagined wealth.

All of these dazzling new developments excite our minds and stimulate our imaginations, giving rise to enormous expectations about the oceanic frontiers of the world. Yet it is true that the richest bounty the sea bestows upon us as human beings is her never-ending power of dynamic recreation. This she does freely, gladly, in generous measure for anyone who will give her opportunity to do so.

The reader may have noticed that the personal pronouns *she* and *her* have often been used of the ocean. For those of us who have come to love her, to live with her, to let her influence us, the sea becomes a living, breathing, dynamic entity in our experience.

This, too, is a part of her gracious glory.

The ocean becomes a friend.

We fall in love with the sea.

She arouses and stimulates the most-profound emotions in our makeup. She inspires our spirits. She energizes our mental processes. She strengthens, heals, and fortifies our physiques. She contributes wholeheartedly and completely to the well-being of our whole person.

It is our awareness of all this, either consciously or unconsciously, that draws millions upon millions of people to seek the seashores of the world every year. They come in hordes, drawn from ten thousand inland towns, cities, and villages, to vacation by or on the ocean. They seek escape, even if only for a few brief days, from the constricting man-made environment of wooden walls, paved streets, concrete canyons, and roaring traffic.

Deep within their souls, there is a subtle yearning, an insistent thirst, a desperate desire to find the space, the serenity, the sweet solace of the sea. Some come just to sunbathe on the beaches or stroll along the sands and cliffs. Others come to swim and surf and water-ski. Some come to snorkel, skin-dive, or search for shells. Some come to sail in the wind, to drift on the tides, or to explore faraway strands. Some come to fish along the shore, to wet a line from a small boat, or to search for the shining monarchs of the deep. Some come just to be alone, in solitude and silence. Some come to enjoy the seascapes, the bird life, and the pungent aroma of the sea.

The result of all this human invasion is the steady growth of a gigantic tourist industry the world around. Huge hotels, lavish resorts, marinas, and visitor facilities of every possible design now dot the shorelines of the world. Out-of-the-way places, which fifty years ago were visited only by daring adventurers or the very wealthy in their private yachts, have become the playgrounds for the proletariat.

A fantastically intricate network of air lines has been flung around the entire globe. Scarcely a single place on the planet has been spared from the ever-widening web of travel facilities, which can take anyone anywhere within a matter of hours for a two-week holiday. A Saint Louis secretary or Chicago banker can be on the shores of Bali or the beaches of Samoa in less time than it takes to drive across their own country.

In terms of time, space, and cost, the travel industry has compressed the earth into a small sphere. Its charms and attractions are available to the masses. The beauties and benefits of its ocean verges are within the reach of anyone prepared to pay a modest sum to relax by the sea. The net result is that many of the more highly advertised spots have become veritable Coney Islands, even in places as remote as Mombasa or Bangkok.

Yet surprisingly enough, for those who may still long for peace, privacy, and solitude, such places can still be found, even in close proximity to some of the largest city centers. It has always surprised and delighted me to discover that there are little bits of beach, corners of seacoast, or secluded strands of sand that somehow have been bypassed by the crowds. Around the world, such spots have enriched my own life in wondrous ways.

Just last week I stumbled across a tough little trail that wound down the face of a steep cliff. It was not the sort of place most people would even think of using to get down to the sea. But, with care and exertion, I climbed gently from the top of the cliffs, to find myself on a sea-swept stretch of glistening white sand. Here the great, gaunt, gray bluffs of basement rock stood like sentinels at the ocean edge. The swirling currents and tidal action of ten million moons had smoothed and polished the rocks where the sandpipers scurried. I had stumbled on a pristine paradise within ten miles of a large population center.

As I strolled along the beach, I stripped off my shirt and trousers, baring my back and legs to the gentle touch of the winter sun. There was not another footprint upon the sand. Only the tiny tracks of gulls, curlews, sandpipers, and godwits were engraved on the shore, and they would be erased by the next high tide.

A sense of excitement gripped my spirit. For me, this was a virgin strand. It lay untouched, untrampeled, unsullied and unmarked by the hand of man. It was precisely as it came from the hand of my Father. It had been shaped and sculpted by the passing of ten thousand times ten thousand tides and storms and seas.

Here the cormorants came to court above the cliffs. Here they nested, generation after generation, upon the ledges of stone whitened with their droppings. Here they raised their broods along the bluffs, with the wind blowing brine and spray across their young.

As my eyes swung in a slow arc from the cliffs to the ocean, I spied several seals sunning themselves on some barnacle-covered rocks. The tide dropped, and more and more of the slick, smooth mammals heaved themselves out of the waves and onto the protruding rocks. The old adults shone dark and almost black. Their younger pups were still garbed in warm, brown, soft coats that shone like bronze in the afternoon light. In quiet contentment, they stretched out in the sun, at peace with the world.

I found a giant driftwood log washed up on the rocks and settled myself to spend a gentle hour of quiet contemplation in this glorious spot. Overhead, great cumulus clouds built castles in the sky as they moved from the sea across the coastal range. The ocean breeze tousled my hair. The call of the curlews sounded across the sands. And I, too, like the seals on the rocks, the cormorants on the cliffs, the sanderlings at tide line, was at peace with life. All was well.

The ocean—this remarkable segment of my Father's world—had once more worked its wonder in my life. At last I rose from my log to start for home. I knew I was richer than when I came. Again, the sea had enriched my days.

This was her great glory. Little wonder

I love her so!

Photographic Notes

The slides for this book were chosen from a collection of several thousand I gathered around the world during the last twenty-seven years.

It has been a monumental task to try and include only those which would best illustrate the text. Often favorite subjects had to be omitted.

Most of them were taken on Kodachrome film, using a Model III F Leica with 50 mm, 90 mm, and 135 mm lenses.

Frontispiece

2 A Pacific sunrise silhouettes the ocean palms in a superb symphony of grace and color.

Introduction
The Pull of the Sea

10, 11 Returning waters cascade back into the ocean on a remote island shore.

1
Wave-Washed Strands and Windswept Sands

2
Sea Cliffs and Rocky Coasts

3
Ocean Islands Under Sun and Rain

4
Wide Skies and Mighty Seas

5
Tide-Line Treasures and Rich Deposits of the Deep

6
Marine Life of a Myriad Sort

7
Man and the Ocean